RETHINKING THE CONTRIBUTIONS OF MAULANA ABUL KALAM AZAD

About the Editor

Ajoy Kumar Chattoraj, an alumnus of Ranchi University, a Gold Medalist of M.A. History of 1973-75 batch, has been teaching History since 1976. He is presently Head, University Department of History, Ranchi University, Ranchi. He obtained his Ph.D. degree from Ranchi University in 1986. He is actively engaged in Research work and has published a number of research papers in different journals.

PREFACE

This book is a collection of papers presented in the National Seminar organized by the Department of History, Ranchi College, Ranchi on March 8-9, 2013, which was sponsored by the UGC, Eastern Regional Office, Kolkata. The theme of the Seminar was *The Role of Maulana Abul Kalam Azad in Indian National Movement and His Contribution in Nation Building.*

Maulana Azad was at once a journalist, a political thinker, a freedom fighter, an educationist and a religious reformist. Maulana Azad stayed in Ranchi during his internment from 5 April, 1916 to 31 December, 1919 and was engaged in social and cultural activities. Maulana Azad's religious ideas were akin to Ashoka or Vivekananda as he stressed on oneness of all religions, which to him was prerequisite to communal harmony. He set an example to honour other religions even sticking to one's own religion. The theme of the seminar was divided in eight sub-themes:

1. Maulana Azad's family background and early life.
2. Maulana Azad as a Journalist.
3. Maulana Azad as a thinker — his social and political ideas.
4. Maulana Azad and Indian freedom struggle.
5. Maulana Azad: Social, political and cultural activities during his internment in Ranchi.
6. Maulana Azad: Ideas about Education and his contribution to the field of Education.
7. Religious Ideas of Maulana Azad and his Spiritualism.
8. Maulana Azad as the maker of Modern India.

This book throws light on his life, ideas, role in freedom struggle, spiritualism, his social, political and cultural activities and his contribution in making India.

Prof. S.Z.H. Jafri traces the influence of Sir Syed Ahmad Khan on Maulana Azad on the question of religion and theology. About social role of religion he was influenced by Jamaluddin Afghani. Maulana Azad's preference to Hindu-Muslim unity to *Swaraj* has been explained by Prof. Jafri. Maulana Azad was a first rate orator. He opposed Sir Syed and everything he stood for in politics. Maulana Azad described the period between 1875 to 1915 as period of wrong leadership and wrong policies. Prof. Jafri traces the origin of Two Nation theory in his chapter.

The role played by Maulana Azad in National Movement and how he conceived India as a secular nation is the theme of Dr. P.K. Shukla's chapter. Maulana Azad understood the problems of Muslims. The most notable contribution of Maulana Azad was to bring Hindus and Muslims on the same platform against the British rule. Dr. Shukla holds the opinion that Maulana Azad saved the Congress from another split following the exit of the *Swarajists* by putting pressure on Congress to allow Pro-Changers to fight Council's election. Maulana Azad urged Muslims to forget Two Nation Theory and enjoy the freedom of the country from foreign rule after India gained Independence.

Dr. L.N. Rana in his chapter focuses on Maulana Azad's activities in Ranchi during his internment from April 1916 to December 1919. Maulana Azad's social and cultural activities in the field of Hindu-Muslim unity, abolition of class and caste distinction, his efforts to educate Muslims have been dealt in details by Dr. Rana. The most remarkable achievement of Maulana Azad in Ranchi was his writings on *Quran* which accorded him as an Islamic scholar in the entire Muslim world. Dr. Rana has also given an account of Maulana Azad's active role in Congress even after India gained Independence.

Dr. Sujata Singh highlights Maulana Azad as a professional journalist. Maulana was involved in journalism from very tender age but he waited till time was ripe for his role to play in Muslim politics at national level. As a journalist Maulana Azad attained tremendous success as he knew to use news for much wider gain in rational way Azad touched upon social problems of contemporary life apart from politics. The article also contains the tributes, editorials and homages that appeared in different newspapers across the world after Maulana Azad's death.

Dr. Anjana Singh in her study objects the claim of a group of Pakistani historians that there had been always two nations in India. She is of the view that Maulana Azad's interpretations of *Quran* and Islam had provided sanctions to his ideas of composite Indian nationalism. She also traces the influence of scholars in the development of his ideas about Islam. His ideas of nationalism and Hindu-Muslim unity have been dealt as well in her chapter.

Dr. B. Rukhaiyar assesses Maulana Azad as an original thinker. Maulana's views on *Khilafat* Movement and Non-Cooperation movement and his efforts to draw Muslims into the mainstream of National Movement are some of the aspects which Dr. Rukhayiar has focused in his chapter. Maulana left no stone unturned to mobilize the Muslim support for Gandhiji's Non-Cooperation Movement. He considers Maulana a practical politician and a farsighted statesman.

Dr. Rashmimala Sahu explains Educational visions of Maulana Azad and its relevance in Modern India. She considers that Maulana tried hard to eradicate illiteracy. He tried to use education as an effective tool for social change and economic growth of India. As a visionary Maulana reshaped, restructured and reorganized the Education system of Modern India. It is to his credit that by introducing Scientific and Technical Education India has found a place among the developed nations of the world.

Shama Sonali's theme is political and social ideas of Maulana Azad. In her chapter Shama stressed the idea of Hindu-Muslim unity as envisaged by Maulana and the part Muslims could play in Independent India. Maulana was critical of Muslim League's separatist politics and he believed that Muslims could play important role in Independent India. Azad's ideas are relevant in contemporary politics.

Hansa Dass interprets certain key concepts of the *Quran* to evaluate his ideas as a progressive scholar of religion in her chapter. It deals in depth about Maulana's interpretation of the concept of '*Tawhid*' in comparison with that of Sir Syed Ahmad Khan and Md. Ali Jinnah. The Concept of Liberalism and Progressivism of Maulana has been highlighted. Maulana remains a symbol of the Muslim will to co-exist peacefully in a religiously diverse country like India.

Ranchi **Ajoy Kumar Chattoraj**
8 May, 2016

ACKNOWLEDGEMENTS

Above all I am thankful to all the contributors whose research papers have been included in this book. I am grateful to the UGC, Eastern Regional Office, Kolkata for their financial assistance to organize the National Seminar. I am obliged to Dr. Meena Soren, Ex. Head of Department of History, Ranchi Women's College and Faculty members of the Department of History, Ranchi Women's College as the seminar was organized in collaboration with Ranchi Women's College.

I am also thankful to Dr. Sudha Sinha, Head of the Department of History, Ranchi College, Dr. Anil Kumar, Assistant Professor, Rajesh Kumar Singh, Assistant Professor, in Ranchi College. I owe a heavy debt to Late Dr. Dilip Kr. Singh, Assistant Professor, Department of Political Science, Ranchi College, Dr. Anjana Singh and Dr. Hansa Dass of Nirmala College, Ranchi for their whole hearted support to make the seminar a success.

I would like to acknowledge the financial support provided by Euro Kids School, Morabadi, Ranchi, the proprietor of Firaylal, Ranchi and the proprietor of Adharsila Structures Pvt. Ltd. without which the publication of this book would not have been possible.

At the end my sincere thanks to students of PG Department, Ranchi College who toiled very hard for the successful organization of the seminar.

Ranchi **Ajoy Kumar Chattoraj**

CONTENTS

		Pages
	Preface	*v*
	Acknowledgements	*viii*
	List of Contributors	*x*
1.	Maulana Abul Kalam Azad and India's Struggle for Freedom *S.Z.H. Jafri*	1
2.	National Movement, Communalism and the India of Maulana Azad (1920-1947) *P.K. Shukla*	12
3.	The Role of Maulana Abul Kalam Azad in Indian National Movement: An Appraisal *L.N. Rana*	21
4.	Abul Kalam Azad: The Making of a Professional Journalist *Sujata Singh*	27
5.	Pan-Islamic Ideas of Nationalist Maulaṇa Azad *Anjana Singh*	41
6.	Maulana Abul Kalam Azad as a Thinker *Banshidhar Rukhaiyar*	47
7.	Maulana Abul Kalam Azad: Educational Vision and Its Relevance in Modern India *Rashmimala Sahu*	54
8.	The Political and Social Ideas of Maulaṇa Abul Kalam Azad *Shama Sonali*	62
9.	Reflections Upon Maulana Abul Kalam Azad's Interpretation of the *Quran* and his Spiritualism *Hansa Dass*	67
	Index	74

LIST OF CONTRIBUTORS

Dr. Anjana Singh, Department of History, Nirmala College, Ranchi University, Ranchi. emal: anjanasingh singh0@gmail.com

Dr. Banshidhar Rukhaiyar, Head of Department, Department of History, Annada College, Hazaribag, Jharkhand. email: bpr.hzb@gamil.com

Hansa Dass, Assistant Professor, Department of History, Nirmala College, Ranchi University, Ranchi. emial: hansadasslsr@yahoo.co.in

Dr. L.N. Rana, Former Professor & Head, Department of History, Ranchi University, Ranchi. email: lnrana@yahoo.com

Dr. P.K. Shukla, Former Member Secretary, ICHR and Fellow, NMM & Library, Teen Murti House, New Delhi.

Dr. Rashmimala Sahu, Senior Asstt. Prof. and Head of Department, Department of Political Science, Nirmala College, Ranchi University, Ranchi. email: sahurashmi09@gamil.com

Prof. S.Z.H. Jafri, Professor, Department of History, University of Delhi, Delhi.

Prof. Shama Sonali, Asstt. Professor, Department of Political Science, Mandar College, Mandar, Ranchi University, Ranchi. email: shamasonali @gmail.com

Dr. Sujata Singh, PG Department of History, Ranchi University, Ranchi. email: drmrssujatasingh@yahoo.com

1

Maulana Abul Kalam Azad and India's Struggle for Freedom

S.Z.H. Jafri

I

Maulana Abul Kalam Azad was a multi-faced thinker and he will be long remembered as one of the leading figures of India's National Movement. He was a profound thinker and interpreter of religion, upholder of secularism, a scholar and journalist, and after 1947 one of the builders of modern Indian state.

First and foremost, he was a scholar of Muslim theology and a highly learned person in all the related fields of Islamic theology. He wrote the famous commentary on *Quran*, though incomplete, still this commentary *Tarjuman-ul-Quran* offers some fresh interpretations specially his interpretation of the Quranic phrase *Zil Kifl* as an allusion to Kapilvastu (the birth place of Gautam Buddha). This became, of course, a talking point among the scholars of comparative religion and theology. It needs to be emphasized that unlike his father Maulavi Khairuddin (himself a scholar of religion but a 'conventional' thinker), he seems to have been less than satisfied with the traditional learning and the 'received wisdom'. It appears that he was influenced by the writings of Sir Syed Ahmad Khan, especially on the question of religion and theology. Going beyond the conventional framework, he began to read English books and Newspapers, having particular interest in History and Philosophy, thus, he was able to combine a sound knowledge of traditional religious studies with a perception of modern ideas and values.

Thus, such a combination created in him an intellectual crisis, something which Maulana Azad never concedes. His thinking on the social role of religion was quite unconventional as he has argued, that:

Religion itself, instead of creating harmony, was the greatest cause of dispute in the social history of man. There cannot be either multiplicity or contradiction in truth. Where there is opposition and dispute there is no dispute.

Such perceptions of religion naturally created an attraction for the person like '*Sarmad*, the person who was put to death for standing against the orthodoxy. Maulana wrote a highly laudatory and complimentary essay on him (AD 1910) and gave the title of *Holy Martyr* (*Shaheed*) and wrote about him that:

> In search for the goal he discarded the distinction between temple and mosque; which person of genuine mystical experience could quarrel with this principle. He added further, '*Sarmad* stood on the minaret of love from which the walls of Kaba and temple appeared of equal height, the flags of belief and unbelief waving together.

Like the intellectual crisis in his faith where he was deeply influenced by the ideas and writings of Sir Syed Ahmad Khan, in the realm of political thinking he was similarly, influenced by Syed Jamaluddin Afghani, whose call for resistance to western imperialism through the instrument of Pan-Islamism. Afghani had specifically excluded India from his Pan-Islamist vision, for this country, he argued, Hindus and Muslims needed to combine together against the British. Later on, a more modernist vision of anti-imperialist resistance was employed by the Young Turks who had seized power in Turkey. Therefore, for him opposing British rule in India and British aggression in Turkey became the major aim of his political strategy. This way he could argue later on for an alliance of Hindu and Muslim nationalists. Defending his participation in *Khilafat* Movement, he made it very clear before the court of law (*Qaul-i Faisal*) that:

> The tenets of Islam are preserved in its scripture. These, under no circumstances, make it permissible for Muslims to enjoy life at the expense of liberty — today the Muslims have come to a firm decision in freeing their country from its slavery, they will take their fullest share along with their, Hindu, Sikh, Parsi and Christian brethren.

Indeed, Hindu-Muslim unity was now to be a cause in itself as the youngest president of the Congress, he claimed in 1923:

> No, my friends, I shall give up *Swaraj*, but not Hindu-Muslim unity

for, if *Swaraj* is delayed it will be a loss for India; but if Hindu-Muslim unity is lost, it will be a loss for whole mankind.

Thus, it becomes clear that intellectual crisis in him led to an unconventional thinking, where the writings of Sir Syed Ahmad Khan exercised great influence on him (it is another fact that later on he became highly critical of Sir Syed's political ideology); while formulation of his political ideology, he became a great admirer of Afghani's suggested course of action for Indians and a more practical approach, he seems to have learned from the experience of the Young Turks. This has made him an anti-imperialist to the core of his heart and a firm believer in the idea of Hindu-Muslim unity for attaining, his primary goal of anti-imperialism.

Then, he was a journalist, having made a mark for himself in the field, for the powerful diction he has employed and the flowery language, with Arabic and Persian phraseology, as its hallmark. His *Al-Hilal* (est. 1912), the circulation of this journal reached at its peak 26,000 copies. Through its column, the message of nationalism was preached with quite boldness, he did not hesitate to evoke the religion in full: the attack on Turkey could be seen as attack on the *khilafat*, the head of world-wide Muslim community. After the outbreak of First World War, the British suppressed *Al-Hilal* in 1915; and its successor *Al-Balagh* which had a very short life. Azad himself was interned at the city of Ranchi and remained here from 1916 to 1st January, 1920.

In addition to these scholarly pursuits for which he is still remembered, a staunch worker and supporter of the Indian National Congress, though in no way its chief ideologue, but still one of the front-ranking leaders of the Congress Party. So much so that he could become President of the Congress twice. Although, a section of the powerful lobby within the Congress had never trusted him, still he could remain a confidant of Mahatma Gandhi and Jawaharlal Nehru throughout. As per his own testimony the Congress Party, by abandoning its earlier commitments, has facilitated the unfortunate partition of the country. His reading of this particular event during the crucial phase of Cripps Mission has always been contested by the spokesperson of the Indian National Congress. Yet he remained, till his death, one of the major Muslim leaders of Indian National Congress. The parliamentary constituencies were selected very carefully to ensure a smooth sailing for him. As the first Education Minister of Independent India, he is credited with numerous institutions for the long-term educational planning like UGC, ICCR, Sahitya Academy and numerous other institutions to promote music and other cultural aspects of India's past.

At the same time he had his critics as well, especially the leaders of Muslim League, who described him as a 'show boy' of Congress Party. The leaders of *Jamiatul Ulema-e-Hind* were also not very appreciative of either his scholarship or his political leadership. Within the Congress Party as well he often faced criticism on the 'communal lines' which peeved him greatly.

II

For a proper understanding of political ideas of Sir Syed Ahmad Khan, especially his apathy with the Indian National Congress can be better understood by taking into consideration the Muslim society in Upper Gangetic valley during the nineteenth century. This became important especially in Bengal Presidency, where the Muslim landed elite, service gentry and the *ma'afidars* have suffered heavily as a result of British policies. They have almost become paupers; it is only one aspect but the class which has benefited most out of these policies was the new middle class consisting of the Bengali Bhadralok. Now, it was this class which came into the forefront of acquiring English education, thus, capturing most of the bureaucratic assignments and purchased maximum *zamindaris* and taking a lead in the political organizations. Therefore, it became necessary to have a quick survey of the ways in which the Muslim elite was marginalized; and also look for the reasons why Sir Syed Ahmad Khan advised the Muslims, first to acquire English education, and then think for any other activity. In the following section an attempt is made to analyze some data (mainly from the English officials) to draw a picture of Muslim elite as it was in the second half of the nineteenth century.

It is perhaps important to point out that the Indian Muslims in Upper Gangetic Valley have faced the brunt of the British repression in the wake of the great uprising of 1857 and even before; especially in Bengal Presidency. No less a person than W.W. Hunter wrote his famous book *Our Indian Musalmans*[1] with the complaint that the '*greatest wrong that the English can do to their Asiatic subjects is not to understand them*'. The data presented by Hunter for Eastern India is quite detailed, and somehow he approaches the grievances of the Muslims quite sympathetically. Though highly critical of the *Wahabi* point of view, he advocates for adopting an attitude of sympathy and concern for the Muslim landed aristocracy, he also pleads with his fellow officers and superiors to adopt such policies which might go against the total alienation of the Muslims from the mainstream.[2]

W.W. Hunter in a very important chapter of the book titled as: *Wrongs of the Muhammadans under British Rule* has given a graphic description of the manner in which the colonial administration has brought *havoc* at the fortunes of the Muslim elite in Bengal and the manner in which the institutions imparting indigenous education were systematically made redundant in one of the regions of the subcontinent with a sizeable Muslim presence. He says:

> 'A hundred and seventy years ago it was almost impossible for a well born Musalman in Bengal to become poor; at present it almost impossible for him to continue rich. . .' for the 'army is now completely closed. No Muhammadan gentleman of birth can enter our regiments. . .'.

He further adds to say that:

> our action has brought ruin upon Muhammadan houses of Bengal. We shut the Musalman aristocracy out of the army because we believe that their exclusion was necessary to our safety. . . .

Similarly, another source of the greatness of Muslim aristocracy was '*their monopoly of judicial, political* or in brief *civil employ . . .*' but as a result of the policies of the government a situation arose where '*there is now scarcely a govt. office in Kolkata in which a Muhammadan can hope for any post above the rank of porter, messenger, filler of the inkpots and mender of pens . . .*'.[3] In fact, Hunter has given complete statistics of the major departments of the government in Bengal for AD 1871, he has shown the negligible number of Muslim employees as against the European and Hindu employees. Similar was the situation in other secular professions like law where the numbers of pleaders of the High Court and the Attorneys have declined over a time, medicine which was never considered as professions worthy of consideration by a high born Muslim, but even in that profession Muslims were to be found very rarely.[4] It has been pointed out by Hunter that such exclusion has partially resulted due to the policy of discrimination practiced by the government against the Muslims. He has quoted from the Government Gazette, a circular from the Office of the Commissioner, Sunderbans, which clearly stated that '*the appointment would be given to none but the Hindus . . .*'. The situation was such that Hunter finally remarks that:

> 'The Muhammadans have now sunk so low that even when qualified for govt. employ, they are studiously kept out of it by government notifications. Nobody takes any notice of their helpless condition, and the higher authorities even do not acknowledge their existence . . .'.[5]

The scenario has changed much before as the infamous *Inam* Commission between AD 1828 to 1846 has already done the damage which has almost uprooted the class of *ma'afidars* (most of them were Muslims and Kayasthas) and had made them almost paupers. The Province of Bengal at the time of colonial government had huge *ma'afi* grants meant to support the religious institutions as well as the institutions of indigenous learning. Fr⊘m the time of Warren Hastings in AD 1772 till AD 1828, it was deliberated in the official circles to start the resumption proceedings and finally in AD 1828, the '*special courts were created, and during the next 18 years the whole province was overrun with informers, false witnesses, and stern pale faced Resumption Officials* . . .'. As a result this gigantic exercise '*an outlay of £ 8,00,000 upon resumption proceedings, an additional revenue of £ 3,00,000, a year was permanently gained by the state . . . a large part of this sum derived from lands held free by Musalmans or by Muhammadan foundations* . . .'. The result of such policies was on the expected lines: '*hundreds of ancient families were ruined, and the educational system of the Musalmans which was almost entirely maintained by rent-free grants received its death blow. The scholastic classes of the Muhammadans emerged from the 18 years of harrying, absolutely ruined* . . .'.[6] The resumption proceedings were fiercest at the beginning, and after languishing for some years, were officially terminated by the government in March 1846. But after quarter a century Hunter recalls:

> The panic of those days is still remembered, and it has left to us a bitter legacy of hatred. Since then, a profession of man of learning, a dignified and lucrative calling under the native rulers has ceased to exist in Bengal. . . .[7]

The situation was not different in other parts of the country as a whole as Sir Syed Ahmad Khan one of the main loyalist of the English had categorically stated that that one of the major causes of the Great Uprising of 1857 was the belief that the colonial government was doing away:

With the study of Arabic and Sanskrit . . . this way the people would be deprived of knowledge of the principles of their own faith and their attention turned to books containing the principles of Christian creed . . .'. it was sought to be done by opening 'missionary schools (where) the principles of Christian Faith were taught'; also 'when the village schools were established the general belief was that they were instituted solely with the view of teaching the doctrines of Jesus.[8]

Given such a background Sir Syed Ahmad Khan, who later on became a great champion for the cause of the upliftment of Muslim education and tried to make the things which could ensure the survival of the Muslim community in the atmosphere of suspicion was opposed to the Muslim participation in Indian National Congress. He had a running debate on the issue not only with the Congress leaders from Bengal but also with the people like Badruddin Tayyabji, who was elected the President of Indian National Congress. This political stand of Sir Syed was always a matter of debate among the leaders of Congress and also in the Nationalist Historiography. A section has never forgotten (or forgiven) Sir Syed Ahmad Khan for taking such a position and hence, they became highly critical of Sir Syed, his policies and last but not least the educational institution he has established. Any such criticism was always taken by Muslim intelligentsia with a pinch of salt it could lent little legitimacy. Hence, Maulana Azad used his powerful literally style to counter the establishment.

III

Maulana Azad's long career as a journalist, as an orator, as a stylist of literary pieces specially his journalistic writings and prison-letters made him almost a cult figure. His firm grip on the matters of Islamic theology, culture and history gave him an opportunity to draw the parallels with the present contexts of the party politics. He could give religious colour to the contemporary problems with such an ease that it became a matter of faith and unbelief (*iman* and *kufr*) to follow a particular strategy of the political parties. An orator of first order he was capable of mesmerizing his audience and thus often provided religious sanctity to the matters of purely political nature.

It is a well-known fact that Sir Syed Ahmad Khan the founder of Aligarh Muslim University was highly suspicious of the activities of Indian National Congress. He considered it as an organization of the

'Hindu Bengalis' and advised the Muslims not to associate themselves with it in any manner. This has made Sir Syed a highly controversial figure not only for the Congress Party but for the Bengali intelligentsia. With Maulana Azad coming closer to the leaders like Aurobindo Ghose and Shyamsunder Chakrabarty during the moment for the annulment of the partition of Bengal, he also joined the *bandwagon* of anti-Aligarh Party. As Mushirul Haque has commented:

> Thus Azad, a product of a family in which every tradition was to be accepted without question, became so radical in politics as to associate himself with one of the important revolutionary (Hindu) leader of Bengal. Gradually, Azad became so much impressed by the activities of revolutionaries that he actually joined the party. It was a difficult task for him because the revolutionaries were exclusively Hindus and actively Anti-Muslim.[9]

Over the period of time Maulana Azad became extremely critical to the policies of Sir Syed and everything for which he stood including the movement for having a charter for Muslim University. He wrote highly critical pieces against this movement, employing the theological arguments and using *Quranic* phrases to dub the movement as suicidal and not serving to the national and Muslim 'cause' at all. By way of illustration the following examples are worth quoting:

(a) When the movement for getting a charter for the university was on, the colonial government had set a pre-condition: for having a corpus fund of rupees thirty lakh in the account of the University. The committee made frantic appeals for raising the corpus funds. It has become such an emotive issue that the women were donating their jewellery for the purpose. Maulana Azad all the power of his pen to oppose the move. He described this movement as *infaq fi sabilis shayateen* and he appealed in the most emotional manner to divert all the funds/money, which has been collected for the corpus fund for the proposed Muslim University charter to be diverted for helping the Ottoman Turks who were fighting a losing battle in the First World War. Crossing the limits of decency, he condemns the proposed university as a *kambakht* and invoked 'the curse of God and his angels on such a university whose thirty lakh rupees is laying in the Indian Banks and Muslim warriors are dying in the snow covered battle fields.' The diction he often implies is most unfortunate, however, when it was suggested that another fund may be raised for sending the medical mission to Turkey he was still critical and wrote most provocative pieces on the issue (*Al-Hilal*, 1st September, 1912, p. 8).

(b) It appears that he was personally against Sir Syed Ahmad Khan for he made very sarcastic and even humiliating personal comments against him. In one of the issues of *Al-Hilal* he began with the *Quranic* anecdote concerning the Prophet Mosses and Pharos of Egypt. Invariably, he brought the story of Samri and allegorically he made it clear that it was nonelse but Sir Syed Ahmad Khan. He always described the period between AD 1875–AD 1915 as the 'period of wrong leadership and wrong policies'. This was an illusion to Sir Syed establishing a school at Aligarh exactly in 1875. Maulana Azad has gone that far to compare this period as the 'forty years period of wandering of Bani Israel'. Such personal comments are really unfortunate.

(c) Sir Syed Ahmad Khan has established Mohamaden Educational Conference (MEC) way back in AD 1886, with the aim of:

(i) to make efforts to introduce Islamic theology as a part of curriculum in the schools established by the government for Muslims.

(ii) to make efforts to introduce western education among the Muslim at the highest level.

(iii) to make efforts to update to revive the indigenous *madrasa* education and to put it at the sound foundation. In addition to these primary aims the conference went on to take up new agendas, basically for the benefit of the Muslims. The sessions of MEC were organized in different parts of the subcontinent and it had the desired impact. For Maulana Azad, the aim of establishing the MEC was to keep the Muslims away from Indian National Congress. And finally, he says that MEC was primarily responsible for keeping the Muslims away from the politics. Again, he uses the *Quranic* verses to justify his argument. In one of the sessions of MEC at Rawalpindi in AD 1915 he got himself invited at the session and made a speech which was aimed at negating whatever impact the Conference was aiming to achieve. Since, then in spite of his efforts, he was never invited for any of the sessions of MEC.

Maulana Azad's writings and speeches had created the impression that he was not only opposed to the political strategy of Sir Syed Ahmad Khan, but was also opposed to Aligarh Muslim University. The majority of the students of Aligarh Muslim University were sympathetic to the policies of Muslim League. Therefore, Maulana Azad was never welcomed at Aligarh. Unfortunately, he was passing through Aligarh sometimes in 1913, the students came to know about the train in which he was travelling, and they reached the station and had hooted him at the platform. This incident Azad could never forget throughout his life.

It was only after Independence that Maulana was invited to deliver the convocation address on 20th February, 1949. He made use of this occasion to raise some of the controversial issues as well. He reiterated that he considered Sir Syed Ahmad's political leadership as the greatest fallacy of his life. He accused the Muslim University for vitiating the communal atmosphere of the country prior to partition and still accused the same policies being adopted at the university. Among the other controversial issues he spoke in favour of adopting *devnagari* script as well along with the Persian script for writing Urdu. He also advocated the study of Hindi classics as a part of Indian heritage. This convocation address was delivered more in the manner of 'victory speech' at an institution which has always been criticized by him.

As per tradition of the university, he was invited by the Student Union in the evening, where the then president of Student Union Mr. Shah Hasan Ata gave a point by point rebuttal to all his accusations, allegations and criticisms of Sir Syed leadership and the same time accused all the political parties as being responsible for the communal divide in the country, which ultimately led to the assassination of Mahatma Gandhi. Naturally, this speech of the president of Union was enough to provoke him, therefore, he left the Union hall making the last remark that 'the future of the student of this university is not as bright as I have thought earlier in my convocation address. You are still in the darkness and shall remain in it for ever'.

It appears that it was more a matter of ego (then perhaps any ideological commitment?) which made him to take such a critical positions and he was consistent in that approach throughout.

REFERENCES

1. W.W. Hunter, *The Indian Musalmans*, 1871, Shimla. However, the reprint of this edition by Premier Book House, Lahore, 1964 has been used here (hereafter Hunter).

2. This becomes the most important interpretation in the twentieth Century nationalist discourse when Maulana Azad reaffirmed the theory of *jehad* in his famous *tazkirah*. This interpretation got full-fledged support by Maulana Ghulam Rasul Mehr who served as the secretary to Maulana Azad as well to develop this interpretation in his monumental Urdu biography of Syed Ahmed of Rae Bareilley after the partition. This understanding remains the most dominant trend in the modern writings especially Urdu historiography. See Marc Gaborieau, The "Forgotten obligation": A Reinterpretation of Sayyid Ahmed Barelwi's *Jihad* in the North-West Frontier. 1826-1831, in *The Resources of History: Tradition. Narration and Nation in South Asia*, ed. Jackie Assayag, Paris-Pondicherry, 1999, pp. 297-98.
3. The chapter suggestively titled as: "The Wrongs of the Muhammadans under British Rule" between pp. 108-162 provides the graphic details of the administrative lapses of the British officials; the policies the British government had adopted which ultimately resulted in the ruin of the Muslim elite in Bengal are discussed in a very loaded manner.
4. *Ibid.*, pp. 125-27.
5. *Ibid.*, p. 131.
6. *Ibid.*, p. 139.
7. *Ibid.*
8. Syed Ahmad Khan, *Asbab-i Baghawat-i Hind*; the Urdu Pamphlet on the *Causes of the Indian Revolt of 1857*, was soon translated into English by authors 'two English friends' who wanted to remain anonymous. It was printed in 1873 and the same has been reprinted with an introduction by Francis Robinson, Karachi, Oxford University Press, 2000. For the specific references, see pp. 16 & 18.
9. Haque Mushirul, *Muslim Politics in Modern India*, Shimla, p. 69.

2

National Movement, Communalism and the India of Maulana Azad (1920-1947)

P.K. Shukla

Maulana Azad (1888-1958) is a national heritage who is remembered in history as a Journalist, a freedom-fighter, a crusader against British imperialism, one of the Chief architects for communal harmony and a Congress Chief who stood like a rock against the partition of the country in 1947. In this chapter an attempt is made to discuss only the role played by Maulana to the struggle for freedom; his contribution to understand the problems of the minorities and finally, how he conceived of India as secular nation.

Maulana was in touch with a staunch extremist Shyamsundar Chakrabarty and Aurobindo Ghose during the *Swadeshi* Movement (1905-1908) when Lord Curzon announced the partition of Bengal.[1] By associating himself with the revolutionaries Azad dispelled doubts from the minds of the people that the Muslims were opposed to the *Swadeshi* Movement.[2] He also succeeded in setting up secret societies in a few towns in North India in order to liberate India from British rule. He did not hesitate to use violent methods to fight against the *firangies*.

Azad was involved in subservice activities during the First World War. He had carried on a 'Pan-Islamist' and anti-British propaganda through *Al-Hilal* and *Al-Balagh*. He defined *Jehad* as fight against injustice. Though he was initially critical of Muslim League, he favoured League's Resolution of 1914 which advocated suitable form of self-government. He encouraged many young students to revolutionary activities. He was in touch with Obeidullah who had escaped to Afghanistan in 1915 and was engaged in doing spadework in India for intensifying revolutionary activity.[3] He gave financial support to some of the conspirators' because of the influence he wielded over the Muslim community in Kolkata. It is therefore, obvious that he was externed from Bengal not because of any incremating articles published in *Al-Balagh* but because of his active involvement in the Silk Conspiracy case and his close association with some of its leaders. He was permitted to stay in Ranchi on the condition that he would stop all political activities against the *Raj*. He had to give guarantee for his behaviour in Ranchi and also the identity of the visitors.[4]

Till 1920 he was not sure to associate himself either with the League or the Congress, although his antipathy to British rule was quite evident. Gandhiji knew his father who supported the movement against racial discrimination in South Africa. In fact Gandhiji wanted to see Azad at Ranchi but the Government disallowed him.

The period from 1919 onwards witnessed a new form of struggle for Independence. Anti-Rowlatt Agitation, *Satyagraha* Movement, Jallianwala Bagh massacre, Martial Law and its atrocities had awakened the country. By then the 'Moderates' in Congress had lost their force and they looked like 'officers without troops'. At the same time Hindu-Muslim unity was at its peak when Hindus and Muslims drank water from the same glass. This unity disturbed the colonial authorities. The confrontation between the people and the government resulted in open clashes. Tagore renounced his knighthood in protest against Jallianwala Bagh massacre, Gandhiji returned his *Kaiser-i-Hind* Gold Medal. The dismemberment of Turkish empire created cause of unrest among the Muslims in India. Azad was deeply concerned about Turkey and her degraded position. His paper *al-Hilal* was banned. He felt attracted to *Khilafat* movement and he plunged into it. Now, with the emergence of *Khilafat* Movement he received institutional support for his own thinking. It was during the Non-Cooperation Movement that he began to bring together the Hindu and Muslim by forming *Ummat-i-Wahidda* (one nation). Thereafter, he became a grand agitator and an ardent spokesman of nationalist cause. It may be noted that from the very beginning Gandhiji had expressed his sympathy for the *Khilafat*. It was in Delhi on January 18, 1920 that he met Gandhiji when he came to Delhi to attend *Khilafat* Conference. Tilak and other Congress leaders were also present. Azad signed deputationist's petition to be sent to Lord Chemlsford, the Viceroy. In their petition the deputation wanted recognition of the Sovereignty of the Caliph. By early 1920 the *Khilafat* agitation gained momentum. The *Khilafat* leaders, Muhammad Ali, Shaukat Ali, Abdul Bari and Azad toured the country, addressed meetings, raised funds and stressed the importance of Hindu support in fighting their cause.[5] Azad regarded it a moral duty on the part of Muslims to defend the *Khilafat* and to save the holy places from falling into the hands of non-Muslims.

In March 1920, 15 Muslims and ten Hindu leaders, besides Gandhiji discussed the Non-Cooperation plan in Delhi. Among the leaders present were Gandhiji, B.G. Tilak, M.M. Malaviya, Lajpat Rai, Dr. Ansari, Ajmal Khan, Maulana Azad, Abdul Bari and Shaukat Ali. Tilak did not support Gandhi's Non-Cooperation, Malaviya expressed reservation, Lajpat Rai supported only the *Swadeshi* part of the movement but Jinnah was opposed to it; he did not want use of religion in politics. Gandhiji warned that Non-Cooperation would be implemented if the Turkish peace terms were not found satisfactory. Gandhiji was supported by Maulana Azad who said that his recent tour of Bihar had convinced him that the Muslims would respond to Non-Cooperation enthusiastically. Although Gandhiji used religious sentiment of the Muslims in the Non-Cooperation movement without antagonizing the non-Muslims in fighting against colonial rule, none of the programmes of the movement include the issue of *Khilafat*. The Non-Cooperation movement, in fact electrified the whole country. It aroused strong sentiments among the people on a wide scale for the liberation of the country. Even the *Jamait-ul-Ulema* called upon the Muslims by the force of a *fatwa* to boycott elections, government schools, colleges and law courts and also renounced titles and ranks. Jawaharlal Nehru had also captured the spirit of the time and said:

> "Many of us who worked for the Congress programme lived in a kind of intoxication during the year 1921. We were full of excitement and optimism and a buoyant enthusiasm. We sensed the happiness of a person crusading for a cause. . . . Above all we had a sense of freedom and a pride in that freedom. The old feeling of oppression and frustration was completely gone."[6]

Azad's remarkable contribution was to bring the Hindus and the Muslims together on the same platform against alien rule. The abolition of the *Khilafat* in 1924 disheartened many Muslims in India but Azad took a pragmatic view of the whole matter. He was of the view that there was an artificial division between spiritual and temporal powers. But the symbol of *Khilafat* that had united the Hindus and the Muslims had now ceased to exist and mistrust and tension between the two communities started growing fast. The so-called felling of Muslims *raj* began to haunt the minds of Hindu communalists who taught that India would be a free nation shortly. The years 1922-24 were marked by the series of communal riots. The *Sudhi Sangathan*, *Tabig* and *Tanzim* movements were launched with the object of converting people from one community to another. In order to tackle the Hindu-Muslim riots and differences between the 'no-changers' and 'pro-changers' a special session of the Congress was convened in Delhi in 1923 with Azad as its President. Azad delivered an eloquent presidential address running into about 43 pages. He offered congratulations to Turkey on her victory and to Mustafa Kemal Pasha for infusing a new spirit among his countrymen. Azad expressed his anguish over communal riots and forcefully attacked the elements that were busy in injecting communal poison into the minds of common people. He said:

> "If an angled were to descend from the high heavens and proclaim from the heights of Qutub Minar to abandon the Hindu-Muslim unity and within twenty-four hours *Swaraj* will be yours. I will refuse the preferred *Swaraj* and not yield on my stand. The delay of *Swaraj* will affect Indians but the end of our unity will be the loss of the entire human race."[7]

He strongly repudiated the Hindu *Sangathan* or Muslim *Sangathan*. He held the view that there was only one *Sangathan* which was the Indian National Congress. He wanted to bridge the gulf between the two rival groups — the 'changers' and 'no-changers'. As a result of Azad's plea, the Congress gave permission to the *Swarajists* — the 'pro-changers' to fight the council's elections and readmitted the followers of Das, Motilal and Vithalbhai Patel to the Congress fold. In fact he saved the Congress from another split.

On the communal issues he took initiative to bring the two factions in a Unity Conference which was held on September 6, 1924 at Delhi under the presidentship of Motilal Nehru. The conference declared that it was not only wrong against law but also against religion for anyone to take the law into their hands, either for the purpose of retaliation or punishment. It was declared that all points in dispute shall be decided by reference either to private arbitration or by reference to the court of law. It was in this conference Azad clarified that cow slaughter was not an integral part of Islam. The conference attended by 300 delegates representing different parties condemned the desecration of places of worship and the use of force for conversion.

But the communal issues were not sorted out. The death of C.R. Das in 1925 was a terrible loss to the country. Das believed that so long as

Muslims were not strongly represented in public life and service, there could be no possibility of Hindu-Muslim understanding. Azad emphasized Das's liberality towards Muslims in Bengal as he offered to reserve 80 per cent of new appointments in Kolkata Corporation.[8]

It is a sad comment on the part of the national leaders that the communal problem could not be solved during 1920s and 1930s. The Nehru Report (1928), Jinnah's Fourteen Points (March 1929), and the All Parties Conference (December 1929), the Simon Commission Proposal (1930) and the three Round Table Conferences (November 1930 to January 1932) could not settle communal problem which in Gandhiji's words became a 'problem of problems'.[9] The basic question was of Muslim representation as a minority in the new constitutional arrangements that were to be made at the provincial and central levels. Most of the historians have generally attributed the partition of India to the failure of Congress-League interim government experiment and the communal riots in 1946 or to Pakistan Resolution of 1940 which made a demand for a separate Muslim Homeland. The failure to form the Congress-League coalition Ministry in U.P. in 1937 is also regarded as a real divide between the Congress and the League which paved the way for the creation of Pakistan. But the crucial period of the late twenties and the early thirties when the seeds of partition were actually sowed is usually ignored. Therefore, the efforts made by Azad in this crucial period for the unity between the parties is worth-remembering.

Azad was a true nationalist. But at the same time he was equally conscious of the problems of the minorities. It may be noted that there has been a failure of the Indian leadership to submit an agreed constitutional plan to Ramsay MacDonald's Award on 16 August, 1932 — which retained separate elaborates and the provision of a Muslim majority in Punjab and Bengal. The Hindu Mahasabha rejected it; the Muslims thought it a distinct-advance, but the Congress adopted a neutral attitude towards it. In such a situation Gandhiji declared "I dare not touch the problem of Hindu-Muslim Unity. It was passed out of human hands and has been transferred to God's hand."[10] Even Jawaharlal Nehru admitted that "there were political reactionaries in the Congress who were 'communalists under National Cloak'."[11] Azad was upset over the Communal Award. But he was deeply concerned about the minority problem. He took initiative of bringing about an agreement among the communities on the communal question and he was supported by Madan Mohan Malaviya and Shaukat Ali. He supported Nehru Report with some modifications. He was instrumental in the establishment of Indian National Union and was the moving spirit behind the formation of All India Nationalist Party. He made serious efforts to negotiate with the League leaders for the settlement of communal issues, but he did not succeed. Since, then he became a confirmed nationalist whose watchwords were freedom, national unity and cultural harmony.

Since, Azad was known for his quite temper, balanced approach to the crisis-ridden political situation, he was called upon to take up the Presidentship of the Congress at Ramgarh Session of 1940. It was not a coincidence that he was elected as President of the INC on 17th March and the Muslim League's Pakistan Resolution of 23rd March, 1940 for a separate homeland. He delivered his speech in chaste Urdu and it was translated into English by Nehru. In his forceful speech he touched upon vital national and international issues including his opposition to declaration of war by Britain without consulting the Congress. While criticizing the British imperialism he said that India did not wish to see British imperialism triumphant and become more stronger delaying the period of Indian subjugation to it.[12] He also covered the communal problem at great length. He admitted its stark reality but also said that it had been created by the British for serving their sinister designs. He said that Hindus and Muslims professed different religious faiths but as nation they were one. They were an integral part of common heritage. He pointed out that there was no contradiction in being and a devout Muslim, in owning the common heritage of Islam and India. On the Hindu-Muslim problem he said:

> "Full eleven centuries have passed by since then. Islam has now as great a claim on the soil of India as Hinduism. If Hinduism has been the religion of the people here for several thousand years, Islam also has been their religion for a thousand years. Just as a Hindu can say with pride that he is an Indian and a Hindu, so also we can say with equal pride that we are Indians and follow Islam."[13]

He dispelled the fears prevalent in the minds of the Muslims and assured that their interests would be protected. He guided the Congress policy throughout its history and said that whatever constitution was adopted for India, there will be the fullest guarantees in it for the rights and interests of the minorities. He did not want that the majority should not decide the interests of the minorities but their interests would depend upon the consent of the minorities.

Maulana Azad admired the virtues of 'composite culture' and condemned the Hindu and Muslim tendency to revive exclusively their own narrow past to the neglect of rich heritage of common culture. Azad believed in non-violence only as a matter of policy, not an article of faith. He justified even the use of armed force for the cause of liberty. In his attitude towards the Second World War, Azad's sympathies were with the Allies who were fighting nazism and fascism. But, Fazlul Haq characterized Azad's presidential address as 'un-Islamic' and said that even in the Punjab and Bengal their position was weak.[14] On the other hand the attitude of the Hindu Mahasabha was equally anti-Muslims. They wanted not only the merger of the Congress with Hindu Mahasabha but also to establish a *Hindu Raj*. Reputing the ideals of the Congress such as *Charkha*, Hindu-Muslim Unity, love and non-violence, the Hindu Mahasabha wanted to organize Hindu-militia-Rama Sena of their own. They wanted to curtail the recruitment of Muslims in the Army. V.D. Savarkar addressed a meeting of the Hindu Mahasabha in Tamil Nadu on March 23, 1940 in which he said '*Swaraj* in India could only be *Hindu Raj*'.[15] In another speech he declared Hindus as a nation. As regards the formation of a national government by the Congress which had a backing of Azad for negotiationing with the British, the remark of Jinnah was very harsh. He condemned this Congress move as a sinister design to establish *Hindu Raj*, although Azad has clarified to Jinnah that it would be composite cabinet and not limited to any single party. Jinnah rebuked Azad and warned him that by saying that he (Azad) was made a Muslim 'show-boy'. He was told by Jinnah that Azad represented neither Muslims nor Hindus and that the Congress was a Hindu Body. Azad repudiated Jinnah's contention of nominating all the Muslims representing Muslim League to the Executive Council as proposed by Wavell in 1945 to resolve Indian problems.[16] He emphasized that to yield to Jinnah's demand would mean reducing the Congress to a communal organization, a position which he was not prepared to accept. Wavell records that in his presence in Shimla, Azad stretched forth his hand to shake it with Jinnah but he refused. By the late 1940s the situation on the communal representation in the interim government and the Constituent Assembly had become worst, particularly when the communal riots flared up in different parts of the country. Within three days of the declaration of 'Direct Action Day' by Jinnah against the formation of Interim government 20,000 people alone in Kolkata were killed and seriously injured. The brutal killings brought the country on the verge of a civil war. The Muslim League had called in *Mullahs* and *Pirs* to protect against the Congress. It has been argued that Nehru's remarks were a direct act of sabotage.[17] Azad's reactions to Cabinet Mission

Plan were completely opposed by Nehru. The fact is that the Congress tried to salvage the situation by issuing certain clarification on the Cabinet Plan but it was too late to have a compromise with the Muslim League.

It may be argued that like most of the Congress colleagues, Azad was firmly opposed to the partition of the country which he thought would create problem instead of solving them. He made it very clear to Wavell that the Congress would not accept parity with the League in the formation of government as this would lead to perpetual conflicts. He wanted an immediate declaration from the government about complete independence with the viceroy remaining only as its constitutional head, particularly when millions of innocent people were being butchered.

To some leaders in the Congress only Ram-Rahim approach could solve the communal problem which was threatening to split the country; to others it was an economic issue requiring long-term action and to some it was struggle for the premier leadership of the country. To Azad who had a clearer understanding of communal politics, the immediate requirement was sharing power with the minorities for safeguarding their interests.

Any discussion would remain incomplete without a word about Azad's famous speech delivered at Jama Masjid after Independence in 1948. After partition the innocent Muslims were at a loss and confused whether to migrate to Pakistan or not. Maulana in his forceful speech asked the Muslims to forget the two-nation theory, which was termed as the death-knell of a life of faith and belief. He urged them to forgo it because the pillars on which they relied were soon to shatter into pieces. He asked them not to migrate to Pakistan failing which the historians would write that they were coward. He once again repeated that the partition of Indian was fundamentally wrong. He blamed the Muslim League for misguiding the Indian Muslims. He urged them to give up the path of vacillation and doubt and enjoy the freedom of country from foreign rule. While reminding the importance of Red Fort he said:

> "Today India is free and you can witness how the flag of free India is waving majestically from the ramparts of Red Fort. It is the same flag which used to be the object of ridicule of the rulers and the butt of their jokes when unfurled earlier."[18]

He asked them not to become escapist and feel afraid of living in this Delhi, which had been nurtured by their blood. While encouraging them to adjust with the changes he said:

"I am not asking you to seek certificates of loyalty out of the fear of the ruling power or to live like camp-followers, as you did during the days of foreign domination. Let me remind you that some of the bright signs and symbols that you discern today in India as a heritage of the past were contributed by your own forefathers. Do not forget them. Do not forsake them. Live like their worthy inheritors. Realize that if you yourself are not willing to run away, no power on earth could make you do so. Come, let us take the pledge that this country is ours, that we belong to it and that fundamental decisions of its destiny will remain incomplete till we participate in them."[19]

REFERENCES

1. *India Wins Freedom: An Autobiographical*, Narrative, Humayun Kabir (ed.), Mumbai, 1959, p. 5.
2. Sumit Sarkar, *The Swadeshi Movement in Bengal* (1903-1908), New Delhi, 1973, pp. 217-43 and 367.
3. *Foreign and Political*, Frontier B-Confidential, A Proceedings, 1914, pp. 24-30. It contains an Appendix to "Silk Letter Conspiracy", quoted in V.N. Datta, *Maulana Azad*, New Delhi, 1990, p. 142.
4. *Home Political*, June 1919, pp. 517-25. After his internment he stayed in Ranchi from December 10, 1921 to January 6, 1923, i.e. for a period of 3 years 9 months. He spent in jail for 9 years 7 months and 24 days. Reference P.N. Chopra, *Maulana Abul Kalam: Unfulfilled Dreams*, New Delhi, 1990, p. 133.
5. Judith Brown, *Gandhi's Rise to Power, 1915-1922*, Cambridge, 1972, pp. 205-06.
6. Jawaharlal Nehru, *An Autobiography*, London, 1955, p. 44.
7. In *Khutbat-e-Azad*, quoted in V.N. Datta, *op. cit.*, p. 129.
8. *India Wins Freedom*, *op. cit.*, p. 25.
9. Mushirul Hasan (ed.), *Muslims and the Congress*, Delhi, 1979, p. 266.
10. *Collected Works of Mahatma Gandhi*, Vol. 32, p. 511.
11. Jawaharlal Nehru, *An Autobiography*, London, 1955, p. 136.
12. *Khutbet-e-Azad*, Malik Ram (ed.), New Delhi, 1981, pp. 2744-75, quoted in V.N. Datta, *op. cit.*, p. 155.
13. *Khutbet-e-Azad*, *op. cit.*, p. 298.
14. For details see *Towards Freedom: 1940* (Part 1), Documents on the Movements for Independence in India (ed.), by K.N. Panikkar, Oxford University Press and Indian Council of Historical Research (ICHR), New Delhi, 2009, pp. 555-57 (pp. 536 to 579 are relevant to understand League's demands).
15. *Towards Freedom: 1940* (Part 1), Document No. 33 (a), *op. cit.*, pp. 585-86. See for details pp. 580 to 603.
16. Ayesha Jalal, *The Sole Spokesman: Jinnah, the Muslim League and the Demand for Pakistan*, Cambridge, 1985, pp. 16-17.
17. Leonard Mosley, *Last Days of the British Raj*, p. 28, quoted in V.N. Datta, *op. cit.*, p. 125.
18. P.N. Chopra, *op. cit.* (Appendix VII), pp. 164-66.
19. *Ibid.*

3

The Role of Maulana Abul Kalam Azad in Indian National Movement
An Appraisal

L.N. Rana

Maulana Abul Kalam Azad (11 November, 1888–22 February, 1958) joined the Indian National Congress in 1920 and actively participated in every direct action launched by the Congress during the course of the Indian Freedom Movement and spent 11 years of his life in British jails. He was a self-made and self-educated man, who grew up in the traditions of an old style theological family atmosphere, but he worked shoulder to shoulder with most advanced modern-minded Indian leaders and made a contribution to the emergence of a free and progressive India. Indifferent to power and wealth and an outstanding scholar of his times, Azad was gifted with an original and creative genius in writing and speech.[1] He repugned imperialism and committed himself unto his last to the cause of Hindu-Muslim unity and advancement of Indian nationalism.

The making of Maulana to greatness began from his early age. He started publishing a monthly *Nairang-e-Alam* in 1899 at Kolkata when he was hardly eleven years old. The periodical carried the poetical collection of the contemporary poets. This was followed by publication of the weekly *Al-Misbah* in 1901 which carried articles on contemporary issues. However, the first major turning point for Azad came after the partition of Bengal in 1905 when he rejected the mainstream of the Muslim middle class, which wanted partition and considered the colonial government as its benefactor.[2] He associated himself with the anti-British movement.

Maulana Azad's visits to France and some Islamic countries in 1908 had a profound and decisive influence on his political thinking. He met the Young Turks, the Arab Natinalists and the prominent leaders of pan-Islamic movement. He also met the Iranian revolutionaries fighting against the Qajar autocracy. The revolutionaries of Islamic countries vividly demonstrated their anti-imperial attitude to Maulana Azad. The writings of Jamaluddin Afghani (1837-1897) also influenced him. He found a new world *astir* with ideas of liberty, progress and revolutionary Islam.[3] Simultaneously, he realized that the Muslim world was facing various kinds of threats from the European countries. Britain was looked upon as an alien power bent upon humiliating Islam in Asia. The contemporary Islamic scenario in India was marked by serious ideological crisis. Sir Syed Ahamd Khan was instrumental in propounding the concept of Islamic modernism in alliance with the British imperialism in Indian subcontinent. On his return to India filled with revolutionary ideas which pervaded the Muslim world, Azad joined hand with Mohammed Ali and Shaukat Ali, Wazir Hasan and others who were opposed to the idea of any alliance with the imperial power.

It was the time when general discontent in India combined with the Muslim resentment produced an explosive situation. At this juncture in June 1912 Azad started the weekly *Al-Hilal* through which he gave fearless and powerful expression to his nationalist ideas. He gave a resounding call for Hindu-Muslim unity through this journal. The basic intent of *Al-Hilal* was to launch a rigorous attack not only on the colonial distortions of our history but also the pro-colonial modernism of Aligarh school, which had poisoned minds of the Muslim intelligentsia. It held out message of nationalism to the Muslim elites and urged them to join other communities in the struggle for the liberation of the country. It was also critical of the Muslim League, its aristocratic leadership and its style of functioning. *Al-Hilal* was regarded by the government as a propagator of dangerous views, especially concerning the war. It led to the forfeiture of the security deposit and in 1914 *Al-Hilal* had to cease publication.[4] The press (*Al-Hilal*) was confiscated in 1915. After five months, Azad started publication of a new weekly under the name of *Al-Balagh*. Its life too was short as its contents were similar to *Al-Hilal*. Ultimately in 1916 the government ordered Azad to leave Bengal under the provision 3A of the Defence of India Act and interned him at Ranchi from where he was released after the war in 1920.

Maulana Abul Kalam Azad stayed at Ranchi from 5 April, 1916 to 31 December, 1919. On his arrival at Ranchi he stayed in local Dak-Bungalow. On 21 April, 1916 he shifted to the residence of Maulvi Abdul Karim, a retired Inspector of Schools, situated in Morabadi.[5]

Later on he was shifted to the house of Sri Chandmal Jain in Upper Bazar. After the Friday prayer in Jama Masjid in Upper Bazar, Azad's discourses on contemporary problems were very impressive and revolutionary in nature. Even some Hindu leaders of the town used to listen to him from outside the mosque.[6]

Maulana Azad's sojourn at Ranchi as an internee is memorable for his social and cultural activities. He developed here very friendly relations with both Hindus and Muslims as Hindu-Muslim unity was his prime concern in the struggle for freedom.

Maulana Azad noticed that the invidious caste-distinction was prevailing among the Muslims of Ranchi. The poor and ignorant weaver community was looked down upon. Marriage of low caste Muslim with high cast Muslim was frowned upon. Azad endeavoured to remove these un-Islamic distinctions. He arranged the marriage of his disciple Imam Ali, a weaver to a high class Muslim girl and himself performed the rite of *Nikah*.[7]

On 15 August, 1917 Azad founded the *Anjuman-e-Islamia* to spread education among the Muslims. In the last week of August *Anjuman-e-Islamia* in the presence of Maulana Azad decided to establish Madarsa Islamia which started functioning at Doranda in a house provided by Munshi Zahoor, from November 1917 with eight students. Azad himself prepared the curriculum entering into its elements of modernism. Shortly a plot of land in Upper Bazar was donated by a *muajjim* of Jama Masjid Sheikh Ziaul Haque for the Madarsa. On this land foundation of the Madarsa was laid by a Hindu — the Chhotanagpur Maharaja on 27 January, 1918 to mark this auspicious occasion a Meeting by well attended Hindus and Muslims both was held, the meeting was addressed by Maulana Azad and on his call Hindus along with the Muslims contributed a considerable amount for construction of the Madrasa building.[8] The Madrasa was shifted to the newly constructed building shortly.

The most remarkable work of Maulana Azad at Ranchi was his writing of *Tarjuman-ul-Quran* which gained him recognition as an Islamic scholar in the entire Muslim world. *Tazkira* was another book written by Azad at Ranchi. It contains a biographical account of his noble ancestors and only a few pages about himself. It is a master piece of elusive style that holds the reader until he gets to the end of the book.[9]

The detention of Azad came to an end on 31 December, 1919. He was released on 1 January, 1920. By this time Gandhiji had emerged as an important leader on the political horizon of India. Azad met him on

18 January, 1920 at the residence of Hakim Ajmal Khan in the presence of Lokmanya Tilak and Ali brothers. He came in close contact with Gandhiji and became prominent among those who supported his Non-cooperation programme for the redress of the *Khilafat* and the Punjab wrongs.[10] He left the Muslim League in 1921 when the League denounced the Non-Cooperation Movement and exhorted the Muslim masses to join the freedom struggles.[11] Chief of the *Khilafat* Committee, the Maulana was also elected President of the special session of the Congress at Delhi in 1923. An ardent protagonist of Hindu-Muslim unity, in his presidential address Maulana Azad said, "If an angel was to descend from the high heavens and proclaim from the heights of the Qutb Minar, discard Hindu-Muslim Unity and within 24 hours, *Swaraj* is yours, I will refuge *Swaraj* but will not budge an inch from my stand. If *Swaraj* is delayed it will affect only India while the end of our unity will be the loss of our entire human world."[12] From this time onwards till the dawn of Independence he remained in the forefront of each subsequent movement and suffered imprisonment every time. At a time when many Indian Muslims led by the Muslim League were crying for partition, he stood up in defence of the unity of the subcontinent. When the Congress launched the Civil Disobedience Movement in 1930 he was arrested.

When the Congress accepted office in 1937, the Maulana, as a member of its Parliamentary Board, guided the working of the Congress ministries. In 1940, he was again elected President of the Congress at Ramgarh session and he continued in this capacity till 1946. In his address to the Ramgarh session, the Maulana denounced the idea of religious separatism and Jinnah's two-nation theory. He wanted a unified nation.[13]

During 1940-1946 Maulana Azad acted as the chief spokesman of the Congress and had negotiations with Cripps in 1942. It was under his presidentship that the historic Quit India resolution was passed at Mumbai. Subsequently, he was arrested along with other leaders and detained in the Ahmednagar Fort. On release in 1945, he participated, as the Congress president, in the Shimla Conference and a year later led the negotiations with the British Cabinet Mission.[14]

A member of the Constituent Assembly, Maulana Azad joined the Interim Government as Minister of Education and Arts. In free India he became the Education Minister and later took charge of the portfolios of Natural Resources and Scientific Research. He was also Deputy Leader of the Congress following the first general election. The Maulana's tenure as Education Minister will be remembered for the University and the Secondary Education Commissions, the reorganization of the All India Council for Technical Education, the rapid development of the Indian Institute of Science, the establishment of the University Grants Commission, the Kharagpur Institute of Technology and the setting up of a chain of laboratories for scientific research throughout the country. A profound scholar, an eminent educationist and a far-sighted statesman, Maulana Azad represented the ideals of secularism and unity in our national life.[15]

Maulana Abul Kalam Azad was one of the towering personalities of modern India. He passed away on 22 February, 1958. On the same day, Nehru in his broadcast to the nation described the Maulana as "the leader of the caravan of the Independence movement in India."[16] He further said "Maulana Azad was 'a great man', a man of luminaries, intelligence and intellect with an amazing capacity to pierce through a problem to its cause. The word 'luminous' is perhaps the best word I can use about his mind. When we miss and when we part with such a companion, friend, colleague, comrade, leader and teacher, there is inevitably a tremendous void created in our life and activity."

Maulana Azad was posthumously awarded India's highest civilian honour, *Bharat Ratna*, in 1992. His Birth Anniversary on 11 November every year is celebrated as 'National Education Day'. Maulana Azad National Urdu University was established at Hydarabad by an Act of Parliament in 1998 for the promotion of higher education with Urdu as the medium of instruction. These steps are fitting tributes by the nation to a person who had unchallenged credentials as a freedom fighter, revolutionary journalist, social reformer, champion of communal harmony and an unparalleled educationist. His prediction on the eve of partition that Urdu speaking Muslims of India leaving for either east or west Pakistan would be marginalized by the local population has come true where we look at the plight of the '*Mohajirs*' in Pakistan and '*Biharis*' in Bangladesh.

REFERENCES

1. Tara Chand, *History to Freedom Movement in India*, Vol. III, Publication Division, Government of India, New Delhi, Reprint, 1992, p. 266.
2. Subhas Kashyap, "Maulana Azad as a Freedom Fighter", www.ummid.com, p. 1.
3. *Ibid.*, p. 3. Also Tara Chand, *op. cit.*, p. 268.

4. Tara Chand, *op. cit.*, p. 269.
5. Jamshed Quamar, *Maulana Azad ka Quyame-Ranchi-Ehwal-O-Aasar*, Maulana Study Circle, Ranchi, 1994. See Appendix — Chronology of Maulana's stay at Ranchi.
6. S.M. Pathak, 'Maulana Abul Kalam Azad in Ranchi', *Journal of Historical Research*, Vols. XXXI-XXXII, 1992, p. 12.
7. *Ibid.*
8. *Jahan-e-Azad*, Special Bulletin, Maulana Azad Study Circle, November 2009, pp. 1-12.
9. S.M. Pathak, *op. cit.*, pp. 13-15.
10. R.S. Sharma, *Makers of Modern India*, ICHR, reprint, New Delhi, 1974, p. 81.
11. Subhas Kashyap, *op. cit.*, p. 5.
12. *Ibid.*, pp. 5-6.
13. R.S. Sharma, *op. cit.*, pp. 81-82.
14. *Ibid.*, p. 82.
15. *Ibid.*
16. Arsha Malsiyani, *Maulana Abul Kalam Azad*, Publication Division, Government of India, New Delhi, 1980, pp. 119-20. See also Mahadeo Desai, *Maulana Abul Kalam Azad: A Biographical Memoir*, Shivalal Agarwal & Co. Ltd., Agra, 1946 for his life and works in pre-Independence India.

4

Abul Kalam Azad: The Making of a Professional Journalist

Sujata Singh

Maulana Abul Kalam Azad is difficult to match in making the legendary combination of an esteemed professional journalist, brilliant orator, highly qualified academician and a sincere politician. Before joining Congress and becoming a part of the *Khilafat* Movement he had had the opportunity of receiving rigorous training and gaining rich experiences in journalism. As early as at the turn of the twentieth century Maulana's articles '*The Art of Journalism*' in *Makhzan* (Lahore) and '*Interesting Information about Newspapers*' in *Lisan us-Sidq*[1] in 1902 and 1904 respectively demonstrate his awareness about the history and role of the powerful medium of newspapers in not only moulding the public opinion but also how it had been put to use in Japan, Europe and America for the national development.[2] According to him a man is always in need of a mentor who would make him aware of dangers ahead. Here, the newspapers as a catalyst has a role to play. As a powerful medium of making changes in public opinion, he made an effort to connect the development of journalism with the process of national development. In this context all issues — social, political and economic — were as important as religious and metaphysical. Moreover, since *Urdu* journalism was still at nascent stage bringing professional approach to it had also become very essential for him. Nonetheless, the young editor Abul Kalam Azad joined active nationalist politics after having been sentenced internment for the aggressive years of journalism that brought him to the limelight and to the notice of Gandhi and an intense bonding and relationship of respect and trust began after his release in 1920.

In Indian context and contradictions between national demand and Muslim politics no doubt Azad did enjoy many identities — a nationalist leader, an authority on issues related to religious matters, champion of communal harmony and most important was his distinctiveness as a journalist. A very apt analysis of forces and times when Azad had to play his role is that "he was pulled into results rather situations which were originating out of conflict between nationalism and colonialism, Islam and colonialism and nationalism and separatism within Muslim politics".[3] Nonetheless, it was his career as a journalist in the beginning of twentieth century which gave him opportunities to put his ideas into practice. The questions emerge, what was the idea behind going for this medium of expression, how far he could achieve, who were his target groups, what was the level of acceptance and rejection was there in an age of radicalism, how strong and convincing his arguments were to separate groups, what innovative technique did he introduce to bring up the standard of journalism, etc. The present chapter is an endeavour to study the journalistic professionalism in the light of present queries.

The multi-dimensional personality of Azad presents a challenge before scholars to capture mannerism of his personality. However, his dynamic persona still is a very relevant to be studied or written about. As Shafey Kidwai writes in a world weary of wars, terrorist attacks, widening disparity, etc. his writings still present a vision of a better world where people are more important than the territories. His autobiographies along with several other writings, speeches and letters create a very useful source material. To name some of them are — *Tajkirah, Ajad ki Kahani Khud Azad ki Jubani, India Wins Freedom,* and *Ghubar-i-Khatir*. The most important in the context of present chapter will be to go through his weekly newspapers like *Al-Hilal* (The Crescent) and *Al-Balagh* (The Preaching). Besides, apart from huge source material available in *Urdu* a plethora of writings and biographies are also available. Mahadeo Desai's *Maulana Abul Kalam Azad*, Humayun Kabir (ed.), *Maulana Azad — A Memorial Volume*, Ian Henderson Douglas' *Abul Kalam Azad: An Intellectual and Religious Biography*, Arsh Malsiyani's *Abul Kalam Azad*, C.P. Sinha (ed.), *Life and Times of Maulana Abul Kalam Azad*, V.N. Datta's *Maulana Azad*, P.N. Chopra's *Maulana Abul Kalam Azad: Unfulfilled Dreams*, Rijwan Kaisar's *Resisting Colonialism and Communal Politics: Maulana Azad and The Making of Indian Nation*, Mushirul Hasan (ed.), *Islam and Indian Nationalism: Reflections on Abul Kalam Azad*, etc. The examination of his early life and family background throws sufficient light on the dominating role they played in the building-up of his character and personality.

Even before his phenomenal rise as editor of *Al-Hilal*, Maulana Azad had an active career in journalism. From a very tender age he had been involved with journals like *Naurang-e-Alam* (1899), *Khadange Najar* (Lucknow), *Makhzan* (Lahore), and weekly *Al-Misbah* in 1901. He could start his paper *Lisan us-Sidq* (Voice of Truth) only in 1904.[4] Even at such a tender age his writing was distinct, forceful and mature.[5] He became the editor of *an-Nadwa* in 1905-06. It was published from Lucknow. However Azad was looking for such opportunities which would give his ideas to reach to a much wider group of readers.[6] The time was also demanding from Azad a more significant role to play in Muslim politics at national level.[7] That is why when he received an offer from *Wakil* which was one of the best known journals published from Amritsar and widely circulated; he joined as editor at an early age of twenty. Most importantly since it was concerned with national problems, Azad had greater scope and opportunities for influencing the public opinion on national political issues through its editorials. He got its circulation farther increased. As long as he remained with it he introduced literary and historical features on regular basis. At the same time he paid serious attention to international issues as well. He wrote about Turkey and Middle East. For a brief period in between he edited *Dar-us-Saltanat*. But by this time due to theoretical differences and personal situation he left *Wakil*.

This brief experience of working for different journals certainly benefited Azad. It reflected in his more mature writing in the editorials of his legendary weeklies *Al-Hilal* and *Al-Balagh* which he started in 1912 and 1915 respectively. The phase was rightly called the 'beginning of more politically oriented phase of his life'.[8] In addition, now he was enjoying the influence over a much wider circle of readers. In fact study Circles were formed where copies of *Al-Hilal* were read out to the member.[9]

However, there were various other reasons which motivated him to go for an *Urdu* journal which could have all the features of modern journalism. In fact according to him, there were many dailies, weeklies and monthlies being published in *Urdu* from U.P. and Punjab where concentration of Muslim population could be found.[10] He had not only worked with many of them but had also been sending articles to reputed papers like *Ashanul-Akhbar* (Kolkata), and *Muraqqua-e-Alam* (Hardoi).[11] Muhamad Ali's *Comrade* and Zafar Ali Khan's *Zamindar* were other leading newspapers.[12] But he was not satisfied with their professional as well as technical standard. "Their get up and printing were as poor as their contents. . . . Nor were they able to print half-tone pictures".[13] That is why he decided that his journal "should be attractive in get up and powerful in its appeal. It must be set up in type and reproduced by the lithographic process".[14] Moreover, content-wise also Azad had a very distinct idea about the kind of role press should have in the context of contemporary political life of people.

The early years of twentieth century was politically ripe enough for many ideologies to take shape at national and international level. India could not escape the impact of such whirl of political activities taking place all around her in pre-World War First scene, i.e. the *Swadeshi* Movement, formation of the Muslim League, the Surat Congress split, the initiation of Indian people into democratic electoral process through Morley Minto Reforms, the Home Rule Movement which consolidated the idea of *Swaraj* in the Indian minds and most importantly the *Khilafat* Movement. In India it was time for distinct identities to grow. Determining position of Indian Muslims and accordingly a role befitting the contemporary situations was badly required. A radical change in the thought process and approach in existing leadership was needed, much different to Aligarh school and traditional *Ulemas*. The handing over political leadership to the affluent people was in the eyes of Azad a theoretical blunder.[15] The point is, the situation had become politically surcharged enough for a journalist like Azad to respond fittingly.

Other developments further confirmed his idea in this regard. He was in touch with revolutionaries of Kolkata who were operating in Bengal and Bihar. The association with extremists Shyamsundar Chakrabarty and Aurobindo Ghose during the *Swadeshi* Movement succeeded to some extent in dispelling the doubts from the minds of people that Muslims were opposed to it.[16] He even tried to intensify a strong revolutionary activity in India in connection with Obeidullah who had escaped to Afghanistan.[17] It is said that his association with the revolutionaries which was earlier 'peripheral' now was strengthened during *Al-Hilal* period (1912-14).[18] After leaving Kolkata he happened to visit many countries like Iraq, Egypt, Syria and Turkey in 1908. All these countries were also going through political unrest of pre-First World War period. He came into contact with the Iranian revolutionaries, followers of Mustafa Kamal Pasha and some Young Ṭurks as well. Young Ṭurks were even publishing a weekly from Cairo to work upon their strategy and it was from here Azad could see how his experience with journalism was going to help in building up public opinion about contemporary issues in India.

The interaction with the Arab and Ṭurk leaders convinced Azad about his earlier beliefs. In India Congress had already become a platform for an organized resistance to British imperialism in India and so far Muslims had remained aloof to such process leading to political inertia.[19] Since, those countries were also fighting against imperialism nonetheless, they failed to understand why Indian Muslim were mere camp followers of the British and in place of leading the national struggle were against the national demand.[20] In fact the Muslim politics was still led by Aligarh school much to the dislike of Azad. Consequently, the goal had now been set-up for Azad. According to him a distinct positive role within the freedom struggle was needed for this, so that, they could not be used by the vested parties. For this Azad decided to create a movement among Indian Muslims on his return to India. According to Humayun Kabir he aspired for nationalism and rationalism in religion.[21] In reality the establishment of *Aqliyat* (rationalism) and introduction of the study of philosophy and science had been his early dreams.[22] However, his approach of interpreting scriptures from a rationalist point of view was criticized by the older conservative leaders.[23]

In this context Gail Minault's observations make sense. While talking about the bearing of Azad's writings on general Indian Muslims he mentions the political and social stress the Indian Muslims were undergoing and were looking for new inspirations, meaning and explanation within religious framework.[24] Actually, he wrote in the ninth issue of *Al-Hilal*, "There will be nothing left with us if we separate politics from religion".[25] But it never meant religious bigotry as he clears, "Islam stands for human freedom and is against tyranny and domination . . . is the spirit of democracy and equality.[26] However, it was considered a radical thinking both religiously and politically at that point of time and quite explosive.[27]

Under these circumstances Azad at the age of twenty four brought a revolution in *Urdu* journalism by establishing *Al-Hilal* Press in 1912. 'Forces of reaction and narrow communalism' could now be campaigned against.[28] Even superior printing and novel ideas had made it an instant success, with the circulation rising up to 26,000 per week within two years. According to Azad, it was a new record for *Urdu* journalism then.[29] In the beginning every new subscriber used to demand all old issues. Nonetheless, the fact that his medium of expression was *Urdu* also bears importance. It contributed greatly in reaching out to millions of people who needed an entirely new approach to understand things around them. The texture of language was concise and was considered a little difficult due to its Persian background. For him photographs, best ink, good printing machines[30] and art of advertisement were key to professional success. He even arranged for action photographs of Turkish war to make news more reliable. The extensive coverage of it had the expected emotional impact on its circulation instantly. According to Gail, the strategy paid well in solidifying Indian Muslim community, a prerequisite for effective political action.[31]

The popularity of his journal not only ensured the reach of Azad's revolutionary ideas to a much larger group every week but equally it had generated reactions from two quarters — the Government and the Aligarh school for different reasons. Both were feeling threatened by the slogan of strong nationalism being preached through his journals. The very leadership of Aligarh school was depended on the Muslims remain loyal to British and thus, be aloof from freedom struggle thereby.[32] The very first issue of *Al-Hilal* wanted people to follow principles of *Quran* and passions for freedom.[33] One of the opinions regarding its phenomenal popularity is, "the opposition to this chapter and the threats to the life of its editor by the followers of Aligarh tradition only made it greatly popular".[34] During this period the Balkan wars were extensively covered by *Al-Hilal* and Azad categorically stated the futility of wars for resolving international issues.[35]

Soon this type of aggressive journalism resulted in Government's wrath by invoking Press Act and a penalty of ₹ 2000 as security. On this occasion he wrote, "The question of *Al-Hilal* and Press Act is the question of Islam and Press Act. The *Al-Hilal* expresses its opinion on a subject according to Islamic principles and does not declare a point which is not based on the *Quran*".[36]

Though both of his journals *Al-Hilal* and *Al-Balagh* were closed by 1916 one by one by the Government under the Press Act, yet, he could not remain away from his journalistic pursuits and soon after his release from the internment in 1920 he asked Malihabadi to work with him for another journal *Paigam*. He took advantage and immediately supported the edict of *Khilafat* Conference at Karachi (1920) to boycott services in the British army in its issue. He reasoned that one should oppose a rule that deny freedom to religion.[37] His arguments were still originating from religious symbolism. But, now he could not have enough time for journalism due to vigorous political career though he kept writing.

The greatest achievement of Azad to *Urdu* journalism was making it more professional by enriching the content. A special feature '*Majakira Ilmia*' (academic discussion) "was introduced to enlighten people about new scientific discoveries, new advancement in social and physical sciences, philosophical debates and the contribution of prominent thinkers and leaders".[38] He published translated news from famous Arabic and English newspapers, i.e. *Alminar, Almureed, The London Times, The Manchester Guardian*, etc. Editorials on various issues were published with relevant questions. Thought provoking articles on matters related to people's life, inviting thinkers for their scholarly writings, etc. were other steps in this direction.

Even the language he used for journalist endeavour has been considered his linguistic contribution to *Urdu*. It gave tremendous thrust to this language to grow as a powerful means of communication of new ideas and thoughts. Modern *Urdu* absorbed many of his new expressions.[39] However, by 1949 due to urgent need for a strong national linguistic unity, he advocated, "every Muslim in India should learn both the scripts".[40] According to him the most virtuous *jihad* is really crusade by language for enjoining good and forbidding evil and not brutal killings.[41]

The writings make his intentions quite clear about what exactly he aimed at with this powerful medium of journalism. He actually had targeted two goals. Firstly, he wanted to 'destroy the obscurantism in the religious life of Indian Muslim' and secondly wished for a joint front of Hindu and Muslim against the British Imperialism and thus to liberate the country.[42] He initiated a dialogue with the readers. It was an effort for collective education and thereby enlightenment. Most important, Azad brought a professional touch by supplementing the so far ignored area of *Urdu* journalism.

As a journalist Azad knew exactly how to use news for a much wider gain in a rational way. Supporting the Turkish cause during pre-First World War period was in reality a part of twin goals. He kept the Muslim community abreast as news from Turkey took enough space in *Al-Hilal* like appealing for funds, and even writing a regular feature column called 'Conditions in Ottoman Empire'.[43] On the other the emotional value of this issue in solidifying the opinion of Indian Muslim community against the British imperialism was evident to Azad. European imperialism was strongly and continuously condemned in his writings leading to forceful and final closure of publication of *Al-Hilal* on November 18, 1914.[44] Obviously, in this way an effective joint political action, in national perspective, could have been possible. During the *Khilafat* Movement one could see the manifestations of his ideology in practice — religious as well as political beliefs in which politics had a well defined place within the religious sphere. Though apparently they seemed to be contradictory but according to him were complementary in nature. He championed the eligibility of *Ulema* to take up the political leadership of the community but he could not accept their obscurantism Western educated group of Indians too were unfit. Douglas, however, finds modification in his ideological framework of expecting theology in politics discourse in post-*Khilafat* days when his stress was more on the historical role of Muslims in India.[45]

However, sometimes the confusion regarding contradictions emerging from his articles had to be clarified to the reader. For this Azad had developed a unique system of educating Muslims on such sensitive issues. He was constantly in touch with his readers through letters. While answering to one such question on religion and politics he wrote, "The question whether political discussion should be separated from religious education is very important. But you must know that this is the very foundation on which we wanted to build the whole edifice of *Al-Hilal*. If you say that the arch is not beautiful we may try to alter its shape, but if you wish that the key stone be removed, then we cannot accede to your wishes. There will be nothing left with us if we separate politics from religion.[46] In fact there were suggestions in several letters written to Azad to look after religious matters only. Azad's emphatic reply to them had always been, "either both or none".[47] In this context Gail Minault analyzes the *Al-Hilal*'s attack on the Government after Kanpur firing on Muslims as one that turned a local issue into a confrontation between Islam and Central Government.[48]

Advocacy of nationalism based on united nationality was another distinguished dimension of Azad's journalistic endeavour and arguments. He vehemently opposed the partition of Bengal which was aimed to weaken the growing spirit of nationalism in the region.[49] In fact, he warned both the Hindu and Muslim minds who intended to surrender the common heritage of 1100 years of living together, "because this notion is wholly unnatural and such thoughts cannot grow in the social reality".[50] He also tried through *Al-Hilal* to convince Muslim leaders like Hakim Ajmal Khan, the Ali brothers and Maulana Abdul Bari of Firangi Mahal, Lucknow regarding the programmes of Non-Cooperation. "I had myself suggested similar programmes in some articles of *Al-Hilal*".[51] With this revelation *Al-Hilal* and *Al-Balagh* become the real forerunner of *Khilafat* in India. He viewed *Wahabi* Movement in a larger perspective of struggle against foreign rule in History.[52]

However, it was much against the existing Muslim politics. In fact, the persuasion of nationalist politics, based on conscious decisions made at the crucial occasions and duly supported by strong ideologies by Maulana Abul Kalam Azad during twentieth century in India, led to the growth of a different kind of politics. "Because I am an Indian, I am a Muslim, I am a human being".[53] Similarly, advocating common nationality of Hindu-Muslim was another dimension of his nationalist approach to fight for freedom during this period. In fact the expression of this unity through his journalism had alarmed the imperial power.[54] At the same time in the very first year of the publication of *Al-Hilal* in 1912 he made it clear that all communities of subject countries, who wanted to be politically free, would have to go through the struggle.

Other issues which found place in his writings were related to political, intellectual and social problems of contemporary life. References from *Quran* were prominently used in his writings while suggesting solutions to various situational concerns. But, whatever subject he dealt with, the element of rationalism always remained in his structure of arguments though sometimes his ideas became quite difficult to comprehend due to extensive use of heavy Persian and Arabic words.[55]

Social issues relating to women also did not escape his attention. He was aware about the contemporary women movements. He published one translation-*cum*-review of Farid Wajidi's book *al-Mar'at-ul-Muslimah* or *Muslim Women, and the Judiciary in Islam* in the journal *al-Nadwa* when he was its editor.[56] He strongly reacted to suicide of a poor Bengali girl of Kolkata named S.H. Debi in March 1914 due to dowry demands. *Al-Hilal* carried an article titled '*A Martyr of Custom*'.[57] A controversy was raised when he pleaded reforms in *Muharram* ceremonies in *Ahsan-ul-Akhbar* that finally led to the closure of this paper.[58] The aim of *Lisan us-Sidq* was to end the superstitions among Muslims.[59] Likewise he stressed on the need for Western secular education in India. Even though he was well aware of practical aspects related to journalism and need for financial independence in a sustained struggle for freedom of expression, he successfully introduced system of advertisement to overcome the financial constraints, but with a professional as well as moral code. Therefore, he never allowed advertising for anything related to gambling, wine or things related to such immoral activities thus managed to arrange the funds for journalism through rightful means.

It would also be interesting to see whether the position which a journalist Maulana had taken on various sensitive issues had changed at any point of time under pressure while being in active politics till last. There had hardly been any change in his views. As for example while discussing the minority position of Muslim in free India there was an apparent continuity in his stand. Long ago in 1912 he considered the unity of Hindu-Muslim as a most essential pre-condition for not only getting Independence but even development of free India would be depending on it. His speeches both at Ramgarh in 1940 and at Aligarh University in 1949 verify that he was quite committed to his belief. Even after the partition in convocation addressed at the Aligarh University on February 20, 1949, he disapproved of the political inertia Muslims had been led into by Syed Ahmad Khan by advising them to keep aloof from the all political movements.[60] Similarly, in 1940 when Jinnah was intending to go for Pakistan Resolution and communal situation had taken for worse he still repeated in his famous Presidential Address in 53rd session of Congress at Ramgarh about the unique position of 80 to 90 million Muslims in India.[61] According to him the cohesiveness of Muslims as a group and their mental and moral qualities put them in altogether a better position in free democratic India than most of other minority groups.[62] Moreover, he remained a solicitous mentor, guardian and friend of forlorn Muslim after the partition, a guarantee of the protection of the rights of Muslims. In reality he deposited before the Cabinet Mission that the partition was to create minorities on both sides introducing a system of mutual hostages.[63]

His writings exhibit that he knew about the numerical strength of Indian Muslims in a parliamentary democratic system as early as in 1912. However, he tried to dismantle the number theory of separatist leadership. He was writing in *Al-Hilal* about this equation of Muslims that was causing fear in their hearts. "Unfortunately, this question of number has become pivot of our political activities. We cannot join the (Indian National) Congress as we are afraid that we (being in a minority) will be swallowed up by the Hindus. We cannot join in the demand for self-government because of the fear that the government will be a Hindu government".[64] Of being majority in five provinces against seven where they were less in numbers and thereby making a minority group, once again he repeated in 1940, "I would remind my co religionist that I stand today exactly where I stood in 1912, when I addressed them on this question of Hindu-Muslim unity . . . I repeat today what I have said throughout the entire period that the ninety millions of Indian Muslims have right course of action except the one to which invited them in 1912". No doubt, he backed up the position he had taken some thirty years ago but there was a little modification in approach. Earlier he was writing with the same maturity which he was showing later on but to get his point home earlier he took advantages of religious symbolism. "As a matter of fact in the eyes of Islam 'number' has no importance at all. . . . Let us not be afraid of Hindus".

Likewise, the nature of Muslim leadership from the very beginning remained subject of sharp criticism, i.e. Western educated Aligarh faction who had formed the Muslim League and religious leader *Ulema*. Commenting on the new emerging leadership in pre-First World War period Gail Minault observes a very new kind of leadership among Western educated Muslims and *ulema* alike who sought to revitalize Muslim cultural and social life but among them the role model was Maulana Azad; part journalist, part orator, and part holy man.[65]

This is quite amazing that the press tributes from Pakistan also took into consideration those certain traits of his personality for which he had remained subject of criticism of majority of Muslims in pre-Independence.[66] According to *The Civil and Military Gazette*, Lahore, "*Al-Hilal* and *Al-Balagh* imparted valuable political education and religious fervour to the rising generation of Muslims and set standard of literary excellence, journalistic ethics and fearless expression of opinion". However, it also added that he had to pay for his convictions along with another journalist Mohammad Ali. Death of a school of thought, reflection of the feelings of Muslim in the columns of *Al-Hilal*, intellectual genius, a crusader against political unconsciousness and religious inactivity, promoter of *Urdu* language as a journalist, maker of *Urdu* journalism and prose — are cbservations sufficient to throw light on the temperament of his writings as a journalist.

The death of Maulana was mourned by people across the world. The leading newspapers of various countries carried special features, tributes, editorials, and homage.[67] It has rightly been observed, "The response of world media was more to a person for whom journalism had been an art and who from the very beginning had realized the significance of journalism as a most effective mode to educate, inform and entertain people from a very early age."[68] He put forward a model of journalism which is not only significant for *Urdu* journalism alone but it enriched the contemporary standard by introducing measurements applicable to one and all. As Shafi Kidwai writes the centrality of his journalism remained a rational truth, having capacity to break the walls between people by opening discourses. But he also evolved techniques to be in constant dialogue with his readers which was essential to make a robust public opinion regarding matters related to different aspects of their life by providing a new language to thought and approach. Though religious and cultural symbols were used in his earlier writings to unite community politically yet as Minault observes it were a quest for pan-Indian Islam, rather than pan-Islamic movement. He remained a practicing journalist and never a passive journalist, reporting news only. For him the role of journalism in one's life should be of a mentor. No wonder, the journalistic writings of Azad in the early years of twentieth century had greatly contributed in making his image as a professional journalist especially after the publication of his journal *Al-Hilal* and though a little debatable statement, still, the 'creation became creator'.

NOTES AND REFERENCES

1. Maulana started a journal *Lisan-us-Sidq* in 1904. The theme of his regular features and critical articles were progress of *Urdu* and social reform. *Bombay Chronicle*, March 20, 1920, as cited in Gail Minault, *The Khilafat Movement*, Oxford University Press, New Delhi, 1982, p. 39.
2. Shafi Kidwai, *The Contribution of Maulana Azad's 'Al-Hilal' in the Awakening of Nationalism in India*, Inaugural Extension Lecture, Centenary Celebrations, Department of Urdu, Ranchi University, 2012, pp. 21-22.
3. Hiranmay Karlekar, "The Nationalism of Maulana Abul Kalam Azad", in Mahavir Singh (ed.), *Maulana Abul Kalam Azad: Profile of a Nationalist*, Anamika, New Delhi, 2003, p. 96.
4. Arsh Malsiyani, *Maulana Abul Kalam Azad*, (Ritat Sarosh, Hindi trn.), The Publication Division, Government of India, New Delhi, 1980, p. 11.
5. Tarachand, *Bhartiya Swatantrata Andolan Ka Itihas*, Part III, The Publication Division, Government of India, New Delhi, 1982, p. 276.
6. Dr. Jakir Hussain authenticates this fact when he paid his tributes to Maulana, "As a student I used to read his *Al-Hilal*. I used to read it aloud to a group of fellow students. It was then that my wick caught fire". *The True Spirit of Religion, in Maulana Azad — A Homage*, The Publication Division, Government of India, New Delhi, 1958, p. 33.
7. Besides political inertia which the Muslim community had been led into by the Aligarh group, the concept of a political party exclusively to look after the Muslim interests, i.e. Muslim League too had been taking shape. The Muslim community had to be motivated in politics with conviction in the right direction at national level.
8. S.B. Singh, "Introduction", C.P. Sinha (ed.), *Life and Times of Maulana Abul Kalam Azad*, K.P. Jayaswal Research Institute, Patna, 1993, p. iv.
9. Mahadeo Desai, *Maulana Abul Kalam Azad: A Biographical Memoir*, Agra, 1946, p. 29.
10. Maulana Abul Kalam Azad, *India Wins Freedom*, Orient Longman, 1989, p. 8.
11. Arsh Malsiyani, *op. cit.*, p. 11.
12. Gail Minault, *op. cit.*, p. 47.
13. Arsh Malsiyani, *op. cit.*, p. 11.
14. *Ibid.*
15. *Al-Hilal*, 18 December, 1912, Kolkata.

16. Sumit Sarkar, *The Swadeshi Movement in Bengal (1903-1908)*, New Delhi, 1983, pp. 217-43 and 367.
17. V.N. Datta, *Maulana Azad*, New Delhi, 1990, p. 142.
18. Rajat Ray, "Revolutionaries, Pan-Islamists and Bolsheviks", in Mushirul Hasan (ed.), *Communal and Pan-Islamic Trends in Colonial India*, New Delhi, 1980, pp. 101-24.
19. *Speeches of Maulana Azad (1947-55)*, The Publication Division, Government of India, New Delhi, 1956, p. 75.
20. Maulana Abul Kalam Azad, *op. cit.*, p. 7.
21. Humanyun Kabir, *Profile of a Scholar Statesman: A Homage*, The Publication Division, *op. cit.*, p. 5.
22. *Lisan-us-Sidq*, August-September issue, 1903 as cited in Jai Narain Sharma, *The Political Thought of Maulana Abul Kalam Azad, Encyclopaedia of Eminent Thinkers*, Vol. XXIX, Concept Publishing Co. (P.) Ltd., New Delhi, 2010, p. 72.
23. Jawaharlal Nehru, *The Discovery of India*, Oxford University Press, New Delhi, pp. 347-48.
24. Gail Minault, *op. cit.*, p. 40.
25. *Al-Hilal*, Vol. 1, No. 9, September 8, 1912, pp. 4-8.
26. *Al-Hilal*, September 1, 1912, Kolkata.
27. W.C. Smith, *Modern Islam in India*, Lahore (reprint), p. 218 as quoted in Mushir-Ul Haq, *Muslim Politics in India*, Meenakshi Prakashan, Meerut, 1970, p. 54.
28. Mahadeo Desai, *op. cit.*, p. 27.
29. Abul Kalam Azad, *India Wins Freedom*, Orient Longman, New Delhi, 1989 (reprint), p. 8.
30. *Al-Hilal*, August 4, 1912.
31. Gail Minault, *op. cit.*, p. 43.
32. The progressive social and religious writings of Sir Syed had inspired Azad. They helped develop the capacity of a community to respond to the challenges of modern age. For details see in Mulana Abul Kalam Azad, *India Wins Freedom*; Mahadeo Desai, *Maulana Abul Kalam Azad*; Arsh Malsiyani, *Abul Kalam Azad.*
33. *Al-Hilal*, 13 July, 1912.
34. Azad, *op. cit.*, p. 7.
35. *Al-Hilal*, 13 July, 1912, Kolkata, p. 21.
36. *Al-Hilal*, 1 October, 1913.
37. Jai Narain Sharma, *op. cit.*, p. 76.
38. Shafi Kidwai, *op. cit.*, p. 25.
39. M. Siddique, "The Work of Maulana Azad", C.P. Sinha (ed.), *op. cit.*, pp. 216-17.
40. *Speeches of Maulana Azad (1947-55)*, *op. cit.*, p. 82.
41. *Al-Hilal*, October 20, 1913, Kolkata.
42. Mushir-Ul Haq, *Muslim Politics in Modern India*, Meenakshi Prakashan, Meerut, 1970, p. 72.
43. Gail Minault, *op. cit.*, p. 43.
44. The security money of *Al-Hilal* was forfeited and a fresh security of ten thousand was imposed and finally its publication was stopped on 18 November, 1914.
45. Ian Henderson Douglas, *Abul Kalam Azad: An Intellectual and Religious Biography*, Gail Minault and C.W. Troll, Delhi, 1988, p. 177.

46. *Al-Hilal*, Vol. I, No. 9, September 22, 1912, pp. 4-8, as cited in Mushir-Ul Haq, *Ibid.*, p. 73.
47. *Ibid.*, Vol. I, Nos. 1 & 9, 1912.
48. Gail Minault, *op. cit.*, p. 47.
49. Maulana Azad, *op. cit.*, pp. 4-5.
50. A.K. Azad, *Musalman Aur Congress* (Urdu), pp. 26-27, as quoted in Tara Chand *op. cit.*, Vol. III, p. 25.
51. Arun Bhatnagar, "Maulana Abul Kalam Azad". *The Illustrated Weekly of India*, 8 October, 1978.
52. *Lisan us-Sidq*, 1904 as cited in C.P. Sinha (ed.), *op. cit.*, p. 51.
53. *Young India*, February 23, 1922.
54. *Ibid.*, p. 9.
55. Jawaharlal Nehru, *op. cit.*, pp. 347-48.
56. Md. Anwarul Haque, "Maulana Abul Kalam Azad: A Family Background and Early Life", C.P. Sinha (ed.), *op. cit.*, p. 31.
57. *Al-Hilal*, March 4, 1914, Kolkata.
58. C.P. Sinha (ed.), *op. cit.*, p. 27.
59. Arsh Malsiyani, *op. cit.*, p. 11.
60. *Speeches of Maulana Azad (1947-55)*, *op. cit.*, p. 75.
61. Mushirul Hassan (ed.), *India's Partition: Process, Strategy and Mobilization*, Oxford University Press, New York, 2001, p. 63.
62. *Ibid.*
63. Mushir-Ul Hasan, *Islam and Indian Nationalism: Reflections on Abul Kalam Azad*, Manohar, New Delhi, 1992, p. 25.
64. *Al-Hilal*, September 1, 1912, Kolkata.
65. Gail Minault, *op. cit.*, p. 45.
66. *Maulana Azad — A Homage*, *op. cit.*, pp. 62-69.
67. *Maulana Azad — A Homage*, *op. cit.*
68. Jayata Singh, *Maulana Abul Kalam Azad as Reflected in Foreign Media*, *Khuda Bakhsh Library Journal*, No. 172, April-June, 2013, p. 1.

5

Pan-Islamic Ideas of Nationalist Maulana Azad

Anjana Singh

> "*The greatest hindrance to human intellectual progress is unquestioning acceptance of traditional belief that the foundation of beliefs should be on knowledge, not on 'taqlid' and inheritance.*"[1]
>
> — ***Maulana Abul Kalam Azad***

Much research on Muslims in India since Independence revolves around partition and their reaction to it. It is majorly an effort to reject the claim of Pakistani historians that the past history of India justifies the claim that there have always been two nations in India, i.e. Hindus and Muslims.[2] The ideological basis of the claim lies on the ground that Muslim Orthodoxy was based on *Ulema* politics and it had exclusively communitarian concerns. Its anti-colonial posture, being grounded in Islamic theology was inconsistent with its essentially secular thrust of Indian nationalism. Much is made of fact that the Muslims more than any other religious entity attached greater importance and value to their religion-cultural habits and institutions; hence they were more prone to being swayed by Islamic rhetoric.

Azad stood as a representative of 60 million Indian Muslims who believed in the tradition of resilience and his concept of composite Indian nationalism. Born in a deeply religious family where every kind of Western idea was anathema, Maulana Abul Kalam Azad was a gifted man who was deeply read in Islamic theology and Persian classics. He was so well-versed in *Sunnat* and *Quran* that he entertained the idea of becoming 'Imam' of Indian Muslims.

Maulana Azad was deeply influenced by the ideas of Jamaluddin-Al-Asadabadi 'Al-Afghani' (1839-1897), since a very young age. Al-Afghani's idea of Pan-Islamism was opposed to the Aligarh school of thought, led by Sir Syed Ahmad Khan. His idioms were echoed in Hali's *Musaddas* in which he advocated co-existence of diverse religious faiths in accordance with that of Prophet Muhammad.[3] Azad met Afghani during his stay in Cairo and Constantinople. He developed the nationalist and anti-imperialist thrust of Afghani's idea in *Al-Hilal*, his Urdu newspaper. Through this Urdu paper he tried to generate religious enthusiasm and political activism among Muslims.

Maulana Azad was able to justify his ideas of Pan-Islamism and nationalism from *Quran* and *Sunnat*. He took his ideas from the holy text and advocated strongly for inter-communal union, citing Prophet Muhammad's covenant with some Jews as historical precedent for an integrated alliance with the Hindus. He imbibed the sentiments of Afghani which said that the substance of Pan-Islamism was to remove foreign domination within the limits of territorial nationalism.

In Azad's perception *Whadat-e-Adyan* (unity of religion) an idea deduced from *Quran*. He quoted verses from holy book that said that Prophets were sent to all communities in all ages, and that the religion they preached were true. The universal message has been communicated to all mankind, but the reason why the religions differ is that they are one in spirit but take different posture in the outward form.[4] This idea was close to the religious ideas of Mahatma Gandhi who believed in the oneness of God. For Azad the religious ideas were more important and the socio-cultural aspect of Islam, so deeply advocated the protagonist of Islam as Iqbal and his ink, were no more than belief of a community.[5] Azad's perception of Islam was more humane. He believed that the most important attribute of God is *ruboobiyat* (nourishment, mercy and justice), which he bestows on all human beings, irrespective of race or community.

Idea of Pan-Islam

Pan-Islamism in India grows slowly between 1908 and 1914 (outbreak of the First World War) as an idea opposed to the dominance of British in the Muslim world. Studies done on the Indian Muslims in the first half of twentieth century by Cambridge University suggests that Pan-Islamic idea grew in India in the period in four strands.

1. The first strand was led by Young Muslims, inspired by Western educated Syed Ahmad Khan and Aligarh Muslims. They include Mohammad Ali, Shaukat Ali, Zafar Ali Khan and others, who brought newspaper as *Comrade, Hamdard, Urdu-i-Mu'alla* and *Zamindar*. In their writings they raised issues of Muslims

across the world and raised concern about war with the Ottoman Empire.

2. Second strand was led at *Al-Afghani* and Maulana Azad who believed that the Muslims should ally with the Hindus, organize politically and revolt against the British. He collaborated with the revolutionary groups of Iraq, Egypt, Syria and Turkey. His paper *Al-Hilal* published anti-Western materials in sympathy with Turkey, which fanned considerable agitation among Indian Muslims. In Kolkata, he set up a number of Pan Islamic societies to propagate these ideas. In fact, *Jamiat-i-Hizb-Allah* (1913) planned to unite Indian Muslims under an Imam (Azad himself) to form an agreement with the Hindus and declare *Jihad* against the British.
3. Third strand of Pan-Islamism was that of the Deobandi *ulemas*, who believed that independence of the Muslim world was necessary of purification and renewal of Islam. As British India was *Dar-ul-Harb*, it needs to be converted to *Dar-ul-Islam*, and for this *Jihad* has to be organized from abroad. This strand was led by Mahmud-al-Hasan, Maulana Husain Ahmad Madni, etc.
4. Fourth strand was that of *Muhajirins* (emigrants) from India who carried out their work in Europe, Middle East and Afghanistan. One group of Indian Muslims went to Oxford, Cambridge and the Inns of Court as Mushir Hosain Kidwai Ajmal al din Mirza and others. The other groups mixed up with Indian revolutionaries as Lala Hardayal and Shyamji Krishna Verma.[6]

As far as the strand of Pan-Islamism of Azad is concerned, the writings of *Al-Hilal* is indicative of the fact that he wanted to bring Muslims generally into politics on the basis of purely Islamic appeal. He himself was consistently clear in his mind that this would happen only with the cooperation of Non-Muslims — A.R. Malihabadi, the faithful disciple of Azad, stayed with him during imprisonment during *Khilafat* and Non-cooperation Movement and has published '*Azad Ki Kahani Azad Ki Zubani*' (1965) and '*Zikr-e-Azad*' (1960). In these books he says that Azad was completely committed to the idea of a united nation, uniting all major religions and all area of India.[7] He strongly believed that God was working through him in quasi-miraculous ways and he wanted him to champion the cause of humanity as perceived in the *Quran*.

Pakistani viewpoint also supports this theory, that Azad played a prominent part in weaning away Muslims from Syed Ahmad's policy of loyalty to the British. K. Sarwar Hasan and Muhammad Ziaul Islam have tried to argue that between 1912 to 1922 Azad showed that his thought was dominated by *Quranic* teachings and political concepts of Islam and ideal state for him was an Islamic state but, his mind changed under the influence of Mahatma Gandhi.[8] This change was largely because the idea of composite nationalism had started taking practical shape in the mind of Azad.

Idea of Nationalism

Maulana Azad got plenty of time to review his thought on nationalism during his internment at Ranchi. *Khilafat* movement was massively supported by all section of Hindus and in United Province at times *Khilafat* committees were undiscernible from the Congress bodies.[9] The situation has established that the ideal of 'Indian nationalism' believed that it is the federative character of nationalism that would concede the distinct identity of 'Indian nationalism' and 'Islamic nationalism' can be interwoven. He believed that it is the federative character of nationalism that would concede the distinct identity of the Muslims. His practical experience that actually began in 1923 made him recognize this fact that the Muslims should participate in the general Indian struggle for Independence.

His idea about himself was that he was an Indian and a Muslim, and the two were mutually strengthening. His school of thought of composite nationalism had placed Indian Islam more firmly in its specific Indian environment. He believed in Gandhi's argument that tolerance was the essence of and integral to Hinduism and Islam.

When Jinnah came up with his idea of Pakistan in 1940, in the same year addressing annual session of Congress at Ramgarh Maulana Azad said:

> "This joint wealth is the heritage of our common nationality and we do not want to leave it and go back to the time when this joint life had not begun. If there are Hindus amongst us, to desire to bring back the Hindu life of a thousand years ago and more, they dream and such dream are vain fantasies. So, also if there are any Muslims who wish to revive the past civilization and culture which they brought a thousand years ago from Iran and Central Asia, they dream and the sooner they wake up the better."[10]

For Azad entire world was creation of almighty and his nation was his mosque and whosoever resided in it was his brother. Hindus as well as Muslims had to understand the rights of the citizen of a common state and his responsibilities. He was one man who was deeply hurt with the decision of partition of India, as it was contrary to the principle for which he stood up all his life. In *India Wins Errors* (1989), Raj Mohan Gandhi says, "Remove him from history and the drama of Hindu-Muslim partnership in the movement of Independence is then robbed of its Muslim protagonist. But this would be a mistake to ignore the reality that for every Maulana Azad and Gaffar Khan there were tens of thousands of Muslims and *Khudai Khidmatgars*."

Conclusion

It may be seen from this standpoint that Maulana Azad's Pan-Islamism and composite nationalism were two faces of the same coin, i.e. Indian Nationalism. Like his counterpart Mahatma Gandhi, he believed in being religiously broad-minded and being true adherent of one's faith, but not in opposition or criticism of the other. It was the thinking of intellectuals as Maulana Azad that Islam in India emerged as more progressive, dynamic, liberal and creative than Pakistani Islam. Maulana Azad's idea of Pan-Islam incorporated nationalist ideals, that enables him to stand amongst the rank of Indian nationalists as Gandhi, Nehru and Patel.

REFERENCES

1. I.H. Douglas, *Abul Kalam Azad — An Intellectual Biography* (ed.), by Gail Minault and Christian W. Troll, Oxford University Press, New Delhi, 1988, p. 76.
2. I.H. Douglas, "Abul Kalam Azad and Pakistan — A Post Bangladesh Reconsideration of an Indian Muslim Opposition", *Journal of American Academy of Religion*, Vol. 40, No. 4, December 1972, Oxford University Press, www.jstor.org/stable/1460895, p. 461.
3. Mushirul Hasan, "Pan-Islamism *versus* Indian Nationalism?: A reappraisal", *Economic and Political Weekly*, Vol. 21, No. 24, New Delhi, 14 June, 1986, pp. 1075-76.
4. Balraj Puri, "Azad and Iqbal: A Comparative Study", *Economic and Political Weekly*, Vol. 31, No. 10, New Delhi, 19 March, 1996, pp. 591-95.
5. *Ibid.*
6. For more on this see K.H. Ansari, "Pan-Islam and the making of the Early Indian Muslim Socialist", *Modern Asian Studies*, Cambridge, Vol. 20, No. 3, 1986, pp. 509-37. Also see Mushir Hosian Kidwai, *Islam and Socialism*, London, 1913 and his *Pan-Islam and Bolshevism*, London, 1937.

7. I.H. Douglas, *op. cit.*, 1972, pp. 462-63.
8. See Mohammad Ziaul Islam, "Transfer of Power in India", *Pakistan Horizon*, Islamabad, Vol. 14, No. 3, Third Quarter, 1961, pp. 233-38. Also see K. Sarwar Hasan, "Abul Kalam Azad on Partition", *Pakistan Horizon*, Islamabad, Vol. 13, No. 4, Fourth Quarter, 1960, pp. 318-23.
9. Mushirul Hasan, *op. cit.*, 1986, p. 1077.
10. Presidential Address of Maulana Azad, Ramgarh, December 1940, in *India Partitioned*, Hasan, pp. 67-68.

6

Maulana Abul Kalam Azad as a Thinker

Banshidhar Rukhaiyar

Maulana Abul Kalam Azad was a thinker par excellence. He was learned in Arabi, Persian, Urdu and English languages. He had a thorough study of the *Quran*. As a journalist he had worked hard from his young age and had developed his opinion on matters of national and religious importance. He fell in love with Urdu poetry at the tender age of twelve and said wonderful *gazhals*. However, the thumping accolades given to the young poet could not retain him to poetry for long as he developed interest in more serious religious and political matters. By the age of twenty he earned for himself an enviable reputation as an orator and translator. These achievements were really surprising, particularly at his young age even though he came from an illustrious family of scholars and religious leaders.

The seeds of an original thinker were always there in him since his early childhood. Born in 1888, he was merely sixteen years old when the Britishers partitioned Bengal in October 1905 on communal lines and created a Muslim dominated province of East Bengal. When the majority of the seasoned Muslim leaders were carried away by the rosy picture of a separate Muslim majority state in the shape of East Bengal, he came up with a note of dissent and opposed the partition of Bengal. He was wise enough from the very beginning to see through the British policy of 'Divide and Rule'. At the same time he was concerned about the problems of the Muslim community in India and abroad.

Like all thinkers, his evolution as a thinker was gradual. His academic training started with an intent to make him a religious leader. It was at this time that he came in contact with modern education after he started reading the articles written by Sir Syed Ahmed Khan. He learnt English language and started reading English newspapers and literature. In his words, "By the time I was fifteen; I started thinking originally and was not ready to accept things as they were taught."[1]

In 1908, he visited Egypt, Turkey and Iraq. He met Iraqi revolutionaries, followers of Mustafa Kemal Pasha and the leaders of the Young Turk Movement. This interaction made him a staunch nationalist. By 1910, he was worried that the Muslims were indifferent to the Indian freedom struggle and was restless to bring them in the national mainstream.

He had a deep and profound knowledge of Arab world. He was concerned about the problems of Muslims in India. He started *Al-Hilal* in 1912 and it raised issues like Muslim University, Trustees of Aligarh Muslim College, etc. It shows the political commitment of *Al-Hilal*. As a literary person, he also started a column on the criticism of Urdu literature in his newspaper and also published *gazhals* and *nazms* in it.

One of the major objectives of *Al-Hilal* was to generate a true interest in the study of the *Quran* and take the true meaning of the *Quran* to the common Muslims. He wrote an essay entitled 'A new path for the study and understanding of the *Quran*', which was published in *Al-Hilal*. In this essay, Maulana Azad expressed his views on the *Quran* in an extensive manner.[2]

In 1914, Abul Kalam Azad founded '*Dar-ul-Irshad*' in Kolkata for the teaching and preaching of the *Quran* and the *Al-Hilal* dated 29th July, 1914 carried the news which highlighted the importance of the foundation of *Dar-ul-Irshad* (Lecture room) and hoped that God will provide everything needed to make it a success.[3] Maulana Azad advocated the foundation of 'Hizbullah' which could serve Islam as per his wishes. Maulana Mehmud-ul-Hasan Deobandi also supported him in his endeavour.

In the meantime First World War broke out and Maulana Azad directed his writings towards exposing the misdeeds of Britain and other Allied forces. At the same time, he kept providing correct information regarding the war policy of the Allied and Axis Powers. He started publishing daily supplementary edition of *Al-Hilal* to update his readers. This antagonized the Britishers and they started looking for an opportunity to harass Abul Kalam. The Britishers soon found an opportunity when the two issues of *Al-Hilal* 14 and 21 October, 1914 were published and carried objectionable articles in the eyes of the Britishers. The English authorities ordered *Al-Hilal* to deposit a security of ₹ 2,000 (two thousand) which was a huge sum in those days. But, Maulana Azad deposited the security and saved the paper.[4]

The question of *Khilafat* proved to be a turning point in the evolution of Maulana Azad as a political thinker. The question of *Khilafat* was a vexed issue as it was a transnational problem. The Indian Muslims were, however, hurt by the humiliating treatment of the Caliph (*Khalifa*) at the hands of the Allied forces led by Britain as they regarded Caliph as their political and religious leader. The nationalist leaders like Gandhiji saw in it an opportunity to win the trust of the Muslims by supporting it. He also hoped that it would make the Muslims join the mainstream of National Movement. Maulana Azad, too supported the cause of *Khilafat*. It is interesting to note that Maulana Azad had opposed the partition of Bengal on communal lines and did not fall in the British trap of segregating Muslims from the mainstream of the Indian National Movement. The *Khilafat* movement proved to be a ridiculous movement as Mustafa Kemal abolished the institution of Caliphate and made Turkey a modern and secular nation. The Indians were fighting for a cause that had lost its relevance in Turkey itself. Maulana Azad, who had a better understanding of the Islamic world in comparison to Gandhiji and others, also failed to realize it. He felt that the *Khilafat* movement was in tune with the Pan-Islamic interests. He said, "If the fight against the Britishers was a *jihad* for Muslims, it was a call of patriotism for the Hindus."[5]

On 25th August, 1921, he read a *Khutba* in the *Khilafat* Masjid of Agra wherein we find his religious belief, political awareness, anti-British sentiments, feelings of Hindu-Muslim unity and unflinching commitment to the cause of Indian Independence.[6]

He took up the cause of the Non-Cooperation Movement as a potent tool to fight the Britishers. It was a tool by which he intended to protect the interests of the Caliph as well as fight for the rights of the Indians. So far the opposition of the British rule was concerned, he had no doubts. He always tried to arrive at a balance between his Pan-Islamic leanings and the interests of the Indian Muslims on one hand and the cause of the Indian freedom struggle on the other. His Pan-Islamic leanings have to be seen in the proper perspective and within the larger framework of Indian nationalism as Muslims constituted an important segment of population in the country. He was very much instrumental in mobilizing the Muslim support for Gandhiji and the Non-Cooperation Movement, though it is equally true that Gandhiji's unconditional support to the *Khilafat* movement had made him an acceptable leader among the Indian Muslims.

Maulana Azad was arrested on 10th December, 1921 and sentenced for one year after a brief prosecution. He wanted to dedicate himself to reading and writing as he was a literary person at heart but it was not to be as he was again called upon by circumstances to take up the responsibility of freedom struggle. He had a clear vision that he had to chart an independent course of action and it is reflected in his actions. Gandhiji and his diehard supporters were not satisfied by the concessions granted by the Government of India Act of 1919 and hence, they decided not to participate in the elections which were to be conducted as per the provisions of the Act. On the other hand, C.R. Das, M.L. Nehru, Azmal Khan, etc. wanted to participate in the elections. Maulana Azad was more concerned about the unity of the warring factions of the Congress than to participate in the elections. It was this farsightedness that made him an acceptable leader and he was called upon to become the Congress President at the young age of 35 in 1923 at the special session of Congress in Mumbai.

Maulana Azad's Pan-Islamic leanings continued side-by-side. In 1925 he was the President of the Central *Khilafat* Committee. The Committee decided to send a delegation to *Hazzaj* under the leadership of Syed Suleman Nadvi. Maulana Azad was not a member of this delegation yet he prepared a memorandum for it.

He thanked in the memorandum Ibn Saud saying he had done a wonderful service to Islam.[7]

Moreover, Ibn Saud was more a champion of modern ideas than the Islamic principles. Similarly, Mustafa Kemal was a man of modern ideas and westernized Turkey after making it a secular republic in 1924. The Indian Muslims went in a delegation to Mustafa Kemal and requested him to either maintain the Caliphate or himself become the Caliph but Kemal spurned the offer. Maulana Azad also had this bent of mind and he could not sense that there was no place for Caliphate when the twentieth century was growing young.

As a nationalist his vision was, however, very clear. He repeatedly asked the Muslims to join the mainstream of the Indian freedom struggle. He also told them that it was the call of Islam to fight for the nation. He believed that Hindu-Muslim unity was very essential and it should be maintained at any cost.

It is not difficult to explain the contradiction in the views of Abul Kalam Azad as he hailed from a family of a reputed Islamic scholars and religious leaders. Also, he failed to realize that the Caliphate had no relevance by then or India could not be brought under the Pan-Islamic umbrella as it had a whooping majority of the non-Muslims or in other words Hindus.

Maulana Azad supported Nehru Report which was opposed by Md. Ali Jinnah. He encouraged Maulana Abdul Razzaque Malihabadi to write in support of Nehru Report and sometimes he himself wrote an article and sent it to him which was published under the name of Malihabadi.[8] He believed that the Hindu-Muslim unity should not be compromised at any cost. The majority of Muslims had turned away from the Congress after the question of *Khilafat* became irrelevant. Maulana Azad was the only towering Muslim leader who was still working hard to bring back the Muslims in the mainstream of national policies. He worked hard to secure the support of Muslims for the Civil Disobedience Movement of 1930. At his persuasion, the Muslims of Bengal, Punjab and the adjoining areas participated in this movement in large numbers. British government was taken aback by the astounding success of the harmless looking salt *satyagraha* and in retaliation declared Congress to be an illegal organization.

Maulana Azad was a practical politician and farsighted statesman. He persuaded Gandhiji and others to take part in the elections of 1937 which were to be held under the provisions of the Act of 1935. He knew that doing so will lead us nearer to the goal of freedom. He played an important role as a representative of the Congress in negotiation with the Muslim League over the formation of the cabinet in the United Province. No breakthrough could be made as the Muslim League was dominated by the landlords whereas the Congress intended to go for agrarian reforms, particularly the abolition of *Zamindari*. This fear was not groundless, the stubborn opposition of the Muslim League to land reforms in the UP during the years 1937 and onwards, proving so clearly enough. The breakdown of these talks did not deter Maulana Azad in his endeavour of Hindu-Muslim unity. He organized a meeting of the *Ulemas* of UP in Allahabad on 17th May, 1937. He persuaded them to leave the Muslim League Parliamentary Board and to go over to the Congress unconditionally. To quote Jaswant Singh "... it was Maulana Abul Kalam Azad who had actually managed this shift of the *Ulemas*".[9] This incident shows his clout as a religious thinker. He was a great scholar and exponent of the *Quran* and *Hadith*. He made efforts, all his life, for the propagation of the real meaning of the verses of the *Quran*. Perhaps no contemporary Islamic scholar made such an effort and with such a regularity to do so. No wonder, he commanded a great respect among the Islamic clerics.

Unfortunately, the Congress could not take full advantage of Maulana Azad's stature as Nehru Committed some mistakes that could have been avoided. Nehru developed inexplicable hostility towards the Muslim League during the election campaign. He told that days of the Muslim League were gone and there was time for direct interaction with the Muslims instead of talking to them through an elitist Muslim organization. This was a premature perception of the situation and harmed the cause of the Indian freedom struggle. Now, the Muslim League hardened its stance unreasonably *vis-à-vis* the Congress. In his autobiography, *India Wins Freedom*, Maulana Azad, who was the President of the Congress from 1939 to 1946, speaking of the aftermath of the 1937 elections, wrote:

> "If the UP League's offer of cooperation had been accepted the Muslim League Party would for all practical purposes have merged in the Congress. Jawaharlal's action gave the Muslim League in the UP a new lease of life. . . . It was from the UP that the League was reorganized. Mr. Jinnah took full advantage of the situation and started an offensive which ultimately led to partition.[10] One of the important fallouts of the formation of the Congress government in states in 1937 was the widening of gap between the Congress and the Muslim League. The Congress realized its folly and started making overtures of friendship to the League. Maulana Azad, too, was anxious about a settlement between the Congress and the League in the interest principally of Congress, but also his own position, because should this feud with the League continue, his own position in the community would . . . become anomalous."[11]

The divide between the Congress and Muslim League kept widening thanks to the machinations of the British. Maulana Azad was very much disturbed. He did his best to wean away the Muslims from the League but failed because the Britishers were patronizing Jinnah and the League. Jinnah hardened his stand on the demand for Pakistan. He was in no way ready for a federation. In reply to Gandhi's question as to what provision for defence and similar matters of common concern he contemplated under the Lahore resolution, Jinnah replied, "There cannot be defence and similar matters of 'common concern' when it is accepted that Pakistan and Hindustan will be two separate, independent sovereign states, except by treaty between the two."[12]

While Gandhiji was prepared to let the Muslim majority areas separate if they wanted to provide a treaty for the satisfactory administration of defence and other matters of 'common concern' to both the parts. Jinnah wanted separation to come first and a treaty for the safeguarding of 'common interest' to India afterwards, on such terms as the two parts might agree to, that is if they could so agree. This, as the then Congress President, Maulana Azad put it, was like 'divorce before marriage'.[13]

However, Maulana Azad always fell in line with Gandhiji whenever differences cropped up. As a thinker, it was a weakness but as a practical politician it was the need of the time. When the Japanese invasion seemed imminent in 1942, there was a difference of opinion between Azad and Gandhiji, but Azad did not oppose Gandhiji in clear cut terms. For example, Azad said: "Gandhiji's prescription is the only alternative; though I doubt its effectiveness."[14] "He suggested no alternative. The events unfolded thereafter differently. Japan was defeated. Moreover, Britain and America came to know of Gandhiji's view that he believed that Japan was going to win and so he entertained the idea that Britain should leave India immediately. Britain denounced Gandhiji as 'a fifth columnist' or a 'quisling' and communicated this message to Roosevelt, the American President."[15]

In spite of these limitations, Azad was an original thinker.

REFERENCES

1. Gubare Khatir, *Abul Kalam*, edited by Malik Ram, Sahitya Academy, 1967, p. 38.
2. Quoted in *Abul Kalam Azad*, Abul Qavi Desnavi, p. 36.
3. *Tarzumanul Quran*, first part, Sahitya Akademy, New Delhi, pp. 550-51 (Quoted in *Abul Kalam Azad*, written by Abul Qavi Desnavi, p. 36).
4. *Ibid.*, p. 39.
5. Sheshadri, H.V., *The Tragic Story of Partition*, Suruchi Prakashan, New Delhi, 1983, p. 78.
6. *Ibid.*, p. 45.
7. *Maqatib-i-Abul Kalam Azad*, Abu Salman Shahjehonpoori, p. 178 (Quoted by Abul Qavi Desnavi in his monograph, *Abul Kalam Azad*, p. 51).
8. *Ibid.*, p. 61.
9. Jaswant Singh, *Jinnah: India-Partition Independence*, Rupa & Co., New Delhi, 2009, p. 217.
10. Maulana Abul Kalam Azad, *India Wins Freedom*, Orient Longman, 1998, p. 171.
11. *Pathway to Pakistan*, Chaudhury Khalliquzamman, p. 182 (Quoted by Jaswant Singh, *Jinnah: India-Pakistan Independence*, Rupa & Co., New Delhi, 2009, p. 244).
12. Jaswant Singh, *op. cit.*, p. 322.
13. *Ibid.*
14. Narendra Singh Sarila, *The Shadow of the Great Game: The Untold Story of India's Partition*, Harper Collins, New Delhi, 2006, p. 127.
15. *Ibid.*

7

Maulana Abul Kalam Azad
Educational Vision and Its Relevance in Modern India

Rashmimala Sahu

Maulana Abul Kalam Azad, the first Union Minister of Education of Independent India was a high profile educationist who has left behind indelible imprints in the educational history of Modern India. To quote K.G. Saiyidain. One of his education secretaries, "Maulana was first and last an educationist. The secret of his success as an educationist lay in the fact that he practiced in his life what he preached in his works. He had the qualities of character and intellect, which he wished to inculcate in the people of his country. His whole life bore a shining stamp of sincerity and truth — truth which he loved and advocated with Socratic passion; truth which makes no compromise with expediency and no concessions to ill-informed criticism or opposition, however bitter it might be." Being a dynamic and visionary educationist, he realized that education could not only eradicate poverty and illiteracy from the country but could also be used as an effective tool for social change and rapid economic growth of our country. Virtually, he played a significant role in reshaping, restructuring and reorganizing the education system of our country. He is regarded as one of the post-Independence architects of modern Indian education system. Thus, his contribution to the field of education is not only massive but also remarkable when viewed in the historical perspective.

Maulana Azad represented a glorious synthesis of cultures, civilizations, thoughts and philosophies which have powerfully influenced India's history. He was a bridge between the old and the new. Indeed he was a strikingly outstanding son of the soil. Born in 1888 in a family of celebrated religious scholars, he was educated at home by his father and men of credit in Islamic learning. He was a learned scholar and a great intellectual. He had a great fascination for Western knowledge even though he strongly opposed Western rule over India. He played a vital role in India's freedom struggle and then in the government of the Indian Republic, remaining a symbol of Muslims will to cc-exist with men of other faiths in modern India. In due course of time, he became one of the greatest scholars in Islamic Theology and Islamic Philosophy. His educational ideas drew their inspiration basically from that source. However, he was equally appreciative of and conversant with other aspect of his cultural heritage — the Indian heritage and the total modern heritage of the age which cuts across the East-West barriers. During his eleven years as Minister of Education, which continued until his death in 1958, he performed a number of important services for Indian education. In order to reorient and reconstruct the education system in the context of a changed perspective, he began his task with a detailed enquiry into the malaise and limitations of the existing educational arrangement by appointing University Education Commission (1948), Kher Committee for Elementary Education (1948) and Secondary Education Commission (1952-53). He followed it with many fundamental policy decisions and establishment of educational institutions which provided firm ground for the development of Indian education system in future.

However, his most significant contribution to education in the post-partition communal violence ridden Indian society has been not in the details of the new pattern of education that was gradually emerging but in the broad democratic, humane, balanced vision, which he brought to bear on the entire structure and content of education. He time and often reiterated the importance of education. He felt that education was "the problem of problems for Asia", and that "one of the surest ways of securing International Peace is fundamental education for the peoples of the world." He especially emphasized 'social education' by which he meant the inclusion of a lively sense of rights and duties of citizenship and the production of an educated mind in the masses in the absence of literary education. This was to include understanding of social conditions of the country, health education, economic improvement through crafts, arts, literature, music, drama, dance, poetry and instruction in universal ethics, including tolerance and mutual appreciation.

Azad was essentially concerned with the basic educational problem of shaping of hearts and minds of his fellow men and women. He devoted himself to the training of individuals who will have the qualities of vision, courage, tolerance and integrity, and to the creation, through them, and for them, of a social order which will be inspired by the ideals of social justice, cooperation, broad mindedness and rationalism. Repeatedly he affirmed in his speeches that the central purpose of our Five Year Plans is not the production of material wealth and resources but the creation of new mind and a new character for which right is more important than the development of agriculture, industry, trade, etc.

Azad never had the opportunity to formally experience the discipline of modern education. It was out of his deep interest in learning and enquiry that he acquired fairly good knowledge of Western Philosophy; read Western History and English literature and was able to comprehend certain principles of popular science. Despite his informal exposure to modern education, one finds in Azad a visionary of modern educational enterprise who laid a strong foundation of a long-term educational and cultural development in India.

Early in his career as a Minister, as he contemplated shaping the future of India through educational policy, he thus envisaged the possibilities: Today India is free . . . she can have any kind of mental mould she pleases. Will it be exclusive . . . or will it be all-inclusive, which has been characteristic of the Indian culture throughout the ages? In the advancement of nations there is no greater hindrance than narrow-mindedness. It is our duty, to keep ourselves free from this disease in the new era of independence. The tradition in India, he said, had been that every kind of culture, every mode of living was allowed to flourish and find its own salvation. He emphasized, the acceptance of unity in diversity has been India's motto throughout the ages. The essence of this principle is a large and wide hearted to toleration in which differences are recognized and given their due. The Indian genius always recognized that truth has many facets and conflict and hatred arise because people claim a monopoly of truth and virtue. Azad wished all Indians to appreciate and imbibe these values which, according to him, should be inculcated through social and general education and in this endeavour he always underlined the critical role of teachers.

Azad's contribution to education can be studied in two distinct categories. One may be the study of his general educational ideas as derived from his basic philosophy of life and the other may be the various educational changes and measures of re-construction which were attempted during his regime with the object of making education adequately responsive to the needs and challenges of the national life.

Vision of Education

Azad was a strong believer in democracy which he thought will take roots and benefit the masses if education is democratized. Democratization of education starts from the perspective of 'achievement orientation'. Azad pinpointed his efforts for the democratization of education through which he wanted to universalize 'achievement' — as the basic criterion in the social selection processes and thereby wanted to break the domination structure of hierarchical Indian society. For this purpose, he emphasized four major programmes: (1) Removal of illiteracy through universalization of elementary education up to secondary standard and a drive for adult education including women education; (2) Equalizing educational opportunities in Indian society where exploitations on the basis of class and caste divisions were rampant; (3) Three-language formulae where the state languages and Hindi would be medium of instruction but English will remain as an important second language; and (4) Sound primary education throughout the country.

Azad viewed, "every individual has a right to an education that will enable him to develop his faculties and live a full human life. Such education is the birthright of every citizen. A state cannot claim to have discharged its duty till it has provided for every single individual means to the acquisition of knowledge and self-betterment". This dream of Azad was finally realized in India when the RTE Act was declared to be a Fundamental Right in India in 2009.

He also held that in Independent India, the planning of education at the National level was even more important than economic or industrial planning. He felt that if educational training was unable to inculcate right values and ideals, the security and welfare of the state would be in jeopardy.

Azad geared his educational policies and actions to the following objectives of Education:

(1) ***Making of Man:*** Azad emphasized on character building education which would help a man to realize his immense potential. The content of education, socializing influences of home and religion and the role of the teacher should aim at building of the character and the choice and the practice of moral and cultural values. He stressed the importance of seven values which contributed to the making of man and his society in pursuit of excellence: (i) The quest of truth is the principal aim of education, but one should not impose one's truth upon

others through violenc a dogmatism; (ii) The concept of justice is another aim c education which is related to appreciation of rights and p..formance of duties as necessary conditions to the discipline of individual and the good of the society; (iii) Spread of enlightenment through right type of education, for true civilization and equality of life; (iv) Lessons of Co-operation and Unity to be learnt through togetherness and friendship paving the way for peace and harmony; (v) The practice of courtesy and chivalry for enriching the quality of life; (vi) Valour and chivalry to be imbibed by the youth through proper training in the school and society; and (vii) Quality of humility which chastens and sustains the spirit of man and the strivings of his mind.

(2) ***Education for Democracy:*** Azad stressed that defences of newly-won freedom which has opened new opportunities had to be built in the minds of free men. This was to be done through Social Education which was accorded a highest priority in his scheme of educational reconstruction. He sets up a section of Social Education in the Ministry of Education in 1948. Linking Social Education with Adult Education he emphasized three aspects: (i) imparting literacy, (ii) inculcating a lively sense of rights and duties of citizenship, and (iii) creating an educated mind in the masses which are deprived of literary education.

(3) ***Education for Development:*** Azad enhanced the role of education in national development and encouraged the growth of science and technology at all levels of education. His vision was to make India self-sufficient in higher technical education to meet all our needs and looked forward to a day when people from abroad will come to India for higher scientific and technical education. He expressed these views while inaugurating the IIT Kharagpur in August 1951. Keeping this in view he reorganized the structure and activities of the AICTE and set-up advanced research Centres in science and technology.

(4) ***Education for National Integration and Secularism:*** One of the cherished objectives of education should be to promote national unity on the basis of a rich diversity of cultures and beliefs. He supported this idea and stressed the importance of textbooks and reading materials in history, civics, geography and literature for promoting nationalism and the idea of unity in diversity. India continues to work on this vision of Azad.

(5) ***Internationalism and Global Citizenship:*** During a function of the Indian National Commission for Cooperation with UNESCO in 1951, Azad expressed the view that Education had a definite role to play in promoting world unity and global citizenship. He believed that the cult of narrow nationalism which was inculcated in many societies conflicted with human progress and human mind should be liberated from prejudice and ill will based on race, class or nationality. This he felt demands changing the entire method of teaching of history and geography in schools.

During the Maulana's stewardship of the Ministry of Education, some massive tasks of fact-finding, stock taking and national planning in the broad fields of education were carried out by Central Ministry of Education. He re-organized the All India Council for Technical Education and saw the establishment of a host of institutions of education and cultural significance including Kharagpur Institute of Higher Technology. the University Grants Commission, the Indian Council for Cultural Relations, Council for Scientific and Industrial Research, Indian Council for Social Sciences Research, the Indian Institute of Science, the National Institute of Basic Education, Central Bureau of Textbook Research, the National Board of Audio-visual Education, the Hindi Shiksha Samiti, the Board of Scientific Terminology for Hindi, Sangeet Natak Academy, Lalit Kala Academy and Sahitya Academy.

Curriculum

Maulana was vividly clear that content and curriculum of education at every level has to be distinctively different from what it used to be in the colonial era and it should address to the objectives of education defined by him and outlined above. He repeatedly stressed following ideas to alter and enrich the content and scope of curriculum —

1. At the elementary level, basic education with its emphasis on learning by doing should form the content.
2. At the secondary stage, curriculum should be re-oriented as proposed by the Secondary Education Commission and should be meant for training in diverse skills and aptitudes and preparation for higher educational pursuits.
3. Educational standards needed to be raised at the university stage and curricula broadened and enriched.

4. Adult literacy and social education programmes should be suitably devised so as to create awareness and productivity.
5. Women education should receive special attention.
6. Physical education, recreation and opportunities for games and sports should form part of educational programmes at all levels.
7. The needs of rural areas with special emphasis on agriculture and craft should receive attention.
8. Suitable textsbooks and teaching and learning material be prepared and attention to be paid on the needs of the handicapped learners.
9. Research and evaluation should test the effectiveness and guide the development of curriculum and programmes.
10. Extensive reforms in examination system to save learners from stress and strain.
11. The curriculum should encourage independent thinking, a sense of judgment and the process of learning how to learn.
12. International cooperation especially under the auspicious of UNESCO should be welcomed and harnessed for the reform of the curriculum.

Teacher and Teacher Preparation

Azad had an instinctive reverence for teachers. He had a firm belief that no reforms in education can be effective without empowering the teachers and no policies can be implemented successfully without taking them fully into board. He described the role of the teachers in the following words: "Ultimately all reforms in education depend upon the quality of our teachers. No changes can be made in education unless there are efficient and devoted teachers to carry them out. Poor wages and loss of social status have been perhaps the main reasons why there has been a fall in the quality of teachers in recent years. You are aware that some measures have already been taken to remedy the state of affairs. I would appeal to them that they must also develop a spirit of real service and dedication in the cause of the nation." He thus stressed the need and significance of training of teachers through training institutes for improving the quality of education.

Challenges

The Constitution of India visualizes a national system of education supported by national policies and appropriate organs of consultation and coordination; but by and large the task of implementing policies depends upon the efforts and resources of the states. Maulana Azad's towering personality and political status helped national planning, but could not ensure the actual implementation of national policies by the state. Though Azad blamed the mechanisms of the state, 'the legacy of the governmental procedures' and the inertia of the machine', for the lack of accomplishment in educational matters, yet he succeeded in registering notable achievements in almost every domain of education which set the tone and direction of educational development in the country in the days to come.

In 2008, Government of India declared 11th November, the day of his birth, as the National Education Day. He has been posthumously awarded India's highest civilian honour, *Bharat Ratna*, in 1992. The eminent educationist and first Education Minister of Independent India died in 1958. It is high time that India recognizes the contributions of Maulana Azad and work on the values the great leader stood for. This is the only path which can help India become the leading knowledge hub of the world in the years to come.

REFERENCES

1. Azad, Abul Kalam (1989) [1958], *India Wins Freedom*, Stosius Inc/Advent Books Division. ISBN 978-0-86131-913-8.
2. Abul Kalam Azad, Syeda Saiyidain Hameed, Mujib Rizvi and Sughra Mahdi, *India's Maulana Abul Kalam Azad* (1990), Indian Council for Cultural Relations.
3. Ravindra Kumar, *Life and Works of Maulana Abul Kalam Azad* (1991), Atlantic Publishers & Distributors.
4. Mohd. Akhtar Siddique (5th August, 2011). *Maulana Abul Kalam Azad: Educational Vision and Contribution*, Internet-Education in India.
5. Nandurkar, G.M. (1981), *Sardar's Letters, Mostly Unknown*, Sardar Vallabhbhai Patel Smarak Bhavan.
6. G. Rasool Abduhu, *The Educational Ideas of Maulana Abul Kalam Azad* (1973), Sterling Publishers.
7. "Visionary Educationist" (7th November, 2010), *The Sunday Tribune-Spectrum*.

8

The Political and Social Ideas of Maulana Abul Kalam Azad

Shama Sonali

Introduction

Maulana Abul Kalam Azad was born on 11th November, 1888 in Mecca into a well educated and elite Muslim family. He was a prominent Indian scholar and a senior political leader of the Indian struggle for Independence. He was a firm believer of Hindu-Muslim unity and believed that Muslims could play a prominent role only in United India. Maulana Azad developed political views which were considered to be radical by most Muslims of the time. He fiercely criticized the British for racial discrimination and stated that the British rule was the main cause of the backwardness and poverty that was being faced by the Indians. He rejected Muslim League's politics of separatism and blamed it for focusing on communal issues rather than on the overall welfare of the Indians. His rebellious nature led him to revolutionary politics in the beginning of the twentieth century and he organized several revolutionary activities in Bengal, Bihar and Mumbai. In 1908 his visits to France, Iraq, Egypt and Turkey had a profound impact on his political thinking. He found a new world that was opening up to the ideas of liberty, freedom, progress and equality that gave his political thinking a new dimension. At this juncture he launched his Urdu weekly *Al-Hilal* in June 1912 at the very young age of 24. He gave fearless and powerful expression to his nationalist ideas through the journal that became an instrument of expression of his ideas for the world.

It is significant to note that all these activities of Azad were prior to the advent of Mahatma Gandhi on the Indian political scene. His meeting with the Mahatma gave him a platform to work for Hindu-Muslim unity and he found institutional support for his political stand. He was largely responsible for drawing more and more Muslims to the folds of the Congress and thus enhanced the momentum of the freedom struggle.

Political Ideas of Maulana Azad

During the pre-Gandhian era, Maulana Azad was very much influenced by the ideas of the West that were being infused throughout the world. Though he received his education in a traditional Islamic manner, his visit to countries like Egypt, Turkey and France made him learn about the modern concepts and ways of education. The ideas of liberty, equality, fraternity and justice influenced his thinking and in India he was very much attracted to the revolutionary movements that were gaining ground in Bengal after its partition in 1905. His radical thinking was very much opposed to the ideas of other Muslim leaders of that time who toed the British line in order to safeguard their interests. He mainly advocated his ideas through his political journal *Al-Hilal* and it became a major instrument to criticize the political philosophy of Sir Sayed Ahmad Khan and the Aligarh School who mainly propagated that Muslims were a distinct and separate community.[1] On the other hand, Azad wanted that the Muslims should be infused with the desire to revolt against the British rule and the oppression that it signified and he also wanted that they should play an important part in the Indian freedom struggle. He was opposed to all forms of communal and separatist politics that was prevalent among the Muslim leaders of that period.

The emergence of Mahatma Gandhi on the Indian political scene in 1915 can be seen as a new chapter and a turning point in the course of Indian struggle for Independence. Gandhiji defined a new beginning and gave new weapons of *ahimsa, satyagraha*, civil disobedience and a stream of politics that was new for the country. He turned the elitist Congress-led struggle to a mass movement with widespread appeal and acceptance. Though, Maulana Azad wanted to meet Gandhiji earlier but could do so only in 1920 in Delhi when he came back from Ranchi where he was interned by the British government.[2] An instant connection was established between the two leaders and the meeting led to a lifelong collaboration. During the *Khilafat* and the Non-Cooperation Movement, Maulana Azad emerged as a prominent Muslim leader of the Congress Party and played an active role in bringing the Muslim masses to the nationalist fold.

His political ideas became clear from his writings in his journal *Al-Hilal* and during his trial before the court during the Non-Cooperation movement he stated that throughout history martyrs have been challenging the foundations of laws and the statutes that are set and established by the illegitimate political authorities and also have played an active role in generating spirit of discontentment against the rulers. Azad said, "The Greek Philosopher Socrates, Jesus Christ and Galileo are some of the great *satyagrahis* who have fought against domination, whether political or religious. The established political regime tries to suppress what an awakened nation considers its birth right. An agitation has been started in India and a tussle is going on between the political rulers and the people who have risen to the recognition of a new sense of honour and dignity. A political regime always tries to justify its subjugation of the subjects. But liberty is the primary right of a man and it is nobody's personal privilege to limit or destroy it. There can be no justification for any political domination over another nation."[3] Islam prescribes that only the sovereignty of God is justifiable and Islam wants to vindicate the rights of man. He states that Islam propounds a philosophy of freedom and democracy. No human being is to be considered the wielder of sovereign authority. A political system can be legitimate only when it gives maximum opportunity to its people so that they can assert the collective national will. If a state limits this opportunity it becomes iniquitous and then the people can revolt against it.

In order to defend the political movement, Maulana Azad brought in the support of Islamic thought and philosophy.[4] He firmly declared that liberty is the natural right of man given by God and no power on this earth has the authority to deny this right. Therefore, political freedom is not only a political duty but a religious act also. His writings are a contribution to political theory in the sense that he has brought out the fundamentals of Islam and connected it to the concepts of democracy and freedom and gives a call to revolt against all the feudal and monarchical elements that are present in the world.[5]

It is also important to note that though Maulana Azad had full faith in the Non-Cooperation Movement and the path that was being showed by Gandhiji, he proclaimed that he differed from him on the question of violence. For Gandhi *ahimsa* was a question of faith but for Azad, Islam did sanction the meeting of violence with violence. But in the context of the political situation in India, he declared that he was committed to *ahimsa* as it was the only course of action that is advisable for the country. He had the courage to speak out of his different views in front of the Mahatma and his writings always depicted his thought process.

Maulana Azad was a champion of Hindu-Muslim unity and wanted that his co-religionists should follow a policy of give and take and both the community members should not follow a rigid approach towards any issue that has an impact on them. He was opposed to all forms of separatist and communal politics that was being followed by the Muslim League. He had full faith in the Hindu-Muslim unity and had a firm belief that both the community had a common destiny. He believed that most of the Muslim leaders were mistaken in approaching the national problem from a communal point of view. The communal problem was very close to his heart and within the framework of the constructive programme he played a vital role in working to achieve the much desired unity between the two communities.[6]

In his book, *India Wins Freedom*, Azad criticizes the partition and declares it to be the most unfortunate event of Indian history. He comes out openly against it and the Congress leaders like Nehru and Patel who accepted the partition. He always was of the opinion that a united India can only suffice to the needs of the Muslims and never supported the Two Nation Theory that was propounded by Jinnah. In the wake of the subsequent massacres that occurred during the partition, Azad believed that the partition created more problems than it solved and said that only British gained from the partition and both the communities lost out to their politics of divide and rule.

Maulana Azad's Social Ideas

As a philosopher and scholar Azad was always sensitive towards the social problems that were being faced by the Indians. He believed that the root cause of many problems were poverty and illiteracy and the caste system that was prevalent within the Hindu community. Like a true Gandhian he believed that untouchability was a national curse and should be done away with as it went against the fundamental principles of equality and liberty. The national struggle for freedom can be won only when these maladies are removed from the society. He also worked for the upliftment of the Muslim masses who were lagging behind due to lack of modern education. Modern education was to work as a tool for their upliftment and progress.[7] Women empowerment was also close to his heart as he believed that strong women can build strong families and a strong nation. In the fold of constructive programme participation of women in the national struggle became a reality and more and more women started coming out of their homes to give a truly nationalist shape to the struggle.

Conclusion

Maulana Azad created a space for himself in the Indian history due to his intellect and sharp thinking and also because of the fact that he was opposed to all forms of exploitation, oppression and injustice. He was among the few Muslim leaders of the time who were above communal and separatist politics. As a leader and President of the Congress in the tumultuous times when the Second World War was going on, he played a vital balancing role within the party and gave a new momentum and direction to the freedom struggle with his able guidance and skill to manage the masses. He was an eloquent speaker and was instrumental in drawing the Muslim masses and especially the youth to the nationalist fold. As a champion of Hindu-Muslim unity he worked endlessly to achieve this goal.

REFERENCES

1. Guha, R., *India After Gandhi: The History of the World's Largest Democracy*, Picador India Publications, Delhi, 2007, p. 6.
2. Pathak, P., "Maulana Abul Kalam Azad and the *Khilafat* and Non-Cooperation Movement (1919-1922)" in Sinha, C.P. (eds.), *Life and Times of Maulana Azad*, K.P. Jayaswal Research Institute Publications, Patna, 1993, pp. 113-15.
3. *Ibid.*, p. 120.
4. Maulana Azad, *India Wins Freedom*, Orient Black Swan, New Delhi, 1959, p. 30.
5. Varma, V.P., "The Political Philosophy of Maulana Abul Kalam Azad" in Sinha, C.P. (eds.), *Life and Times of Maulana Abul Kalam Azad*, K.P. Jayaswal Research Institute Publications, Patna, 1993, pp. 528-30.
6. *Ibid.*, p. 534.
7. Anupam, A., *Indian National Movement and Maulana Abul Kalam Azad*, Khudabaksh Oriental Library Publications, Patna, 2007, pp. 272-75.

9

Reflections Upon Maulana Abul Kalam Azad's Interpretation of the *Quran* and his Spiritualism

Hansa Dass

Maulana Abul Kalam Azad was not only a stalwart of the Indian National Movement but also a liberal scholar of religion. The chapter studies Maulana Azad's translation and interpretation of certain key concepts of the *Quran* to evaluate his ideas as a progressive scholar of religion. He has presented an Urdu translation of the *Quran* and has styled it the '*Tarjuman-al-Quran*' which has been edited and rendered into English by Dr. Syed Abdul Latif. This is the main source used for the chapter. Maulana Azad has rendered his "Urdu translation in three volumes — '*Surat-ul-Fatiha*', '*Muqaddana-i-Tafsir*' and '*Tafsir-al-Bayan*'. For the purpose of the chapter, certain key concepts have been picked up from the Commentary of the '*Surat-ul-Fatiha*' as the '*Surat-ul-Fatiha*' in itself has been taken to be the '*Umm-ul-Quran*' or Core of the *Quran*. The chapter has been arranged in three sections. The objective of the chapter is to study in Section I how Maulana Azad has interpreted the three main attributes of God — '*Rububiyat*', '*Rahmat*' and '*Adalat*'. He explains '*Rububiyat*' as Divine Providence which establishes God not only as the Creator of the Universe but also as its nourisher and sustainer. '*Rahmat*' he explains as an act of mercy which God bestows upon the Universe and in '*Adalat*' or Divine Justice he dwells upon God's accounting for the actions of men on the Day of Recompense. An attempt in this section is also made to evaluate Maulana Azad's interpretation of the concept of God or '*Tawhid*' and his focus upon "Unity in Attributes". Section II compares Azad's interpretation and concept of '*Tawhid*' with those of Sir Syed Ahmad Khan and Muhammad

Ali Jinnah. A study of religions into which mankind was divided at the time of the delivery of the *Quran* has also been made in this Section. Section III discusses how Maulana Azad considers the '*Din*' of God as the Straight Path to bring together humanity and restore unity. The chapter concludes that Maulana Azad's concept of liberalism and progressivism can well be attributed to an open and rational view of the Holy Book.

SECTION I

The beauty of the world is a manifestation of God's attributes. Besides being the Creator of the Universe, Allah is also its nourisher. This is what is meant by Divine Providence or '*Rububiyat*'. Hence, the word '*Rabbol-Alamin*' or the '*Rabb*' used for God. Maulana Azad has tried to interpret '*Rububiyat*' in the context of this nourishing and sustaining of the world by Allah. According to him, the best example of '*Rububiyat*' could be seen in the nursing of a child by the mother. When the child is small, the mother feeds and nurses it. But as the child grows, mother's love, though does not die, gets subsided because now this grown-up child is able to take care of itself. This is '*Rububiyat*' or Divine Providence. The mother takes care of the child when it needs it but once on its own, her love though does not finish, subsides. This is the actual meaning of '*Rububiyat*' — that God provides to man all that he needs, but according to the situation and stage he is in. This is Allah's "nourishment" or "sustenance". God showers his '*Rububiyat*' on men and animals and on the entire nature equally. Here, Maulana Azad considers the difference between '*Rahmat*' and '*Rububiyat*'. '*Rahmat*' is an act of mercy on the part of God and '*Rububiyat*', his effort to sustain this mercy. Hence, whatever we see in the universe, owes its existence to Allah's '*Rububiyat*' and whatever there is in the world, has some purpose or other to serve. In this context, the *Quran* talks about '*Takhliq-bil-Haq*'. Maulana Azad dwells upon the inner aspect of '*Rububiyat*' which he classifies into '*Taqdir*' and '*Hidayat*'. '*Taqdir*' assigns a particular role to every object in the world and '*Hidayat*', by means of instinct and perception, shows it the path to follow.

The second important attribute of God which Maulana Azad discusses is '*Rahmat*'. The qualities of love, compassion, benevolence and generosity constitute his '*Rahmat*'. That is why Allah has also been called *Al-Rahman* and *Al-Rahim* and whatever beauty or perfection there is in the world, is an expression of God's Divine Benevolence or '*Rahmat*'. For example, the beauty of flowers, water, clouds, pearls, etc.

Maulana Azad attempts to relate God's '*Rahmat*' with the theory of Survival of the Fittest — in that '*Rahmat*' falls only upon those objects in life which are good, useful and true. And therefore, whenever there is a conflict between '*Haq*' and '*Batil*', i.e. truth and falsehood, success always rests with '*Haq*'. This is known as the decree of Truth or '*Qada Bil-Haq*'. And so, God has also been called *Al-Haq*, the Ever True and the Everlasting. The *Quran* is always for goodness and against wickedness. But at the same time, the *Quran* places a vast and limitless emphasis upon forgiveness. The importance of God's '*Rahmat*' can be judged by its mention in more than 300 places of the *Quran*. Maulana Azad has drawn attention upon the use of the word '*Kasab*' in the '*Surat-ul-Fatiha*', i.e. what one has to enjoy or bear in consequence of the acts performed by him. This is Allah's Divine Justice or '*Adalat*'. Allah is the 'Master on the Day of Recompense' or '*Malik-i-Yawmiddin*'. This justice is aimed at introducing a balance in the world which has been called '*Qaiman-bil-Qist*'.

Maulana Azad has tried to highlight the concept of God or '*Tawhid*' in the *Quran* and says that initially, God was visualized in respect of awe and terror because man could not understand the hidden beauty of the universe and in most cases, was bound to be affected more by the destructive aspect of nature than by its constructive aspect. This led him to visualize God as terror and not love. But a change came over gradually and man began to understand the attributes of mercy and beauty embodied in God. The *Quran* embodies a comprehensive concept of the Unity of God. It emphasizes not upon anthropomorphism but upon transcendentalism. Only the attributes of God are personified and image worship is not allowed. There was no idea of God representing terror but was seen as an embodiment of mercy and beauty. Maulana Azad points out that the idea in vogue before the delivery of the *Quran* was that God was one, i.e. it presented a positive side of the unity of God. This was known as "Unity in Essence". The *Quran* postulated "Unity in Attributes", i.e. apart from the idea of unity of God, another side was presented and that was — God alone, and no one else, is worthy of worship. There is a verse in the '*Surat-ul-Fatiha*' which says, "Thee alone do we serve and from Thee alone do we seek aid", laying great emphasis upon "Thee alone". The *Quran* attributes another quality to God — Divine Guidance or '*Hidayat*'. Men as well as lower animals are guided by the '*Hidayat*' by instinct and sense. But there is a third kind of '*Hidayat*' found only in men — this is the '*Hidayat*' of reason. But the greatest gift to mankind is the '*Hidayat*' of revelation.

SECTION II

By way of examining Maulana Azad's interpretation of '*Tawhid*' or concept of God, it is necessary to put forward the interpretation and concept of '*Tawhid*' in view of religions into which mankind was divided at the time of the delivery of the *Quran*. An attempt is also made here to assess the interpretation of '*Tawhid*' by two leading intellectuals, Sir Syed Ahmad Khan and Muhammad Ali Jinnah.

At the time the *Quran* was delivered, there were five leading religions which had their own interpretations of the concept of God — the Chinese, the Indian, the Magian, the Judaic and the Christian. Among the Chinese, polytheism was the popular faith and God was seen as a Celestial Being — an expression of both beauty and terror. In Hindu ideology, the *Upanishads* presented a pantheistic view of life and God was seen as Light, Perfection, Beauty, the Almighty, the Most Merciful and the Most Loving, and the object of true love and affection. The early Brahmanic religion was succeeded by Buddhism which possessed no concept either of God or of the soul. Its doctrines dealt only with goodness in life and freedom from it and emphasized upon '*Ashtanga Marga*'. In the Magism of Iran, supernatural power was divided into deities who brought love and happiness, and those who worked havoc in human life. Zoroaster rescued the people of Iran from the clutches of Magism and placed its belief on '*Ahura Mazda*' — the God and '*Angrame Niyush*' — Satan. In Judaic concept, the relation between God and man was seen to be that between husband and wife, in which the husband would not tolerate the wife's infidelity. Christianity brought with it a new message — God was seen as an embodiment of love, mercy and forgiveness.

An analysis of Sir Syed Ahmad Khan's religious views calls for an attention to the very fact of his allegiance to the British. He has been considered to be a foremost statesman and Muslim reformer of the nineteenth century. He felt that it is the will of Allah that British became masters over India. It is the mercy of Allah on Muslims for which they must thank Allah. It also appears that his religious views were bound by his personal opinion and his intention of serving his own personal political objectives. So far as the *Quran* is concerned, Syed Ahmad Khan is said to have rejected *Hadith* and *Tafsir* and has been accused of making '*Taweel*' or creating hidden meaning. He seems to have his own version of '*Tawhid*'. According to him, those who do not believe in God at all are not *mushrik* and will still go to paradise. He stated that those who do not have religion, also have a religion and that is Islam. Syed Ahmad Khan seems to have denied that religion has any role in worldly affairs. He created a new philosophy and called it Naturalist. Upon '*jihad*', Syed Ahmad Khan said that Islam forbids Muslims from invading any country and to forcibly spread Islam.

Muhammad Ali Jinnah, on the other hand, believed in one Supreme God and one mankind without any distinction of high and low and without any discrimination on the basis of religion, caste, creed, race or colour. In fact, his views on different subjects of state and society show that he had a deep understanding of the principles of the *Holy Quran*. But while Syed Ahmad Khan believed that religion had no role in worldly affairs, Jinnah asserted that Islam actually gives a complete code of life and it is not only religion, but it contains laws, philosophy and politics as well. He asserts that in the *Quran*, Islam is always refereed to as '*Din*', i.e. a complete code of life and not as '*Muzdhab*' (the Arabic word for religion). This mixing up of religion and politics had obvious political implications for the country.

Quite differently, Maulana Azad has considered God in the context of "Unity in Attributes". He talks about a conflict between '*Haq*' and '*Batil*', i.e. truth and falsehood, and says that every man has to account for his good or bad deeds. Allah favours '*Haq*' and only true persons could have the *Rahmat* of Allah. Also regarding Paradise and Hell, Maulana Azad held that the *Quran* states that an individual's lifespan is divided into two periods — one which concerns with life in this world, and the other covers the life after death. The result of good action is good and that is reward. Similarly, the result of an evil action is evil and that is punishment. The one is designated heaven and the other, hell. The *Quran* says that the inmates of the fire and the inmates of Paradise are not to be held equal and that the inmates of Paradise only shall be the blissful.

SECTION III

Maulana Azad's interpretation of the *Quran* reveals his line of thought and establishes that the roots of progressivism and liberalism that he represented, could be found in an open and rational view of the Holy Book itself. His method of presentation is simple and direct and he has tried to restore the simplicity of the *Quran* which according to him was forgotten in earlier interpretations of the Holy Book. Maulana Azad has tried to impart an explanation of the *Quran* which in his own words had adopted an alien colour due to flawed interpretations. He has attributed this deterioration in the approach to the meaning of the *Quran* to a gradual decadence in the quality of the Muslim mind itself and that the standard of the *Quran* was brought down. Maulana Azad also accuses earlier interpretations of the *Quran* of '*Tafsir-bir-rai*', i.e. commentary which sought to establish the writer's personal views. Thus, in the preface to the first edition of the '*Tarjuman-al-Quran*', he clearly states that his aim is to furnish a self-explanatory translation of the *Quran* in Urdu, to convey the sense of the original in full.

Maulana Azad, emphasizing upon the idea of unity of God, asserts that the teaching of one religion endorses the teaching of another. The *Quran* itself states that all revealed religions present but one and the same basic message. Despite this, the form of worship in one religion differs from the other. The reason he says is that every religion has both spirit and an outward manifestation. The spirit is called '*Din*' and the outward manifestation of the religion is called '*Shar'a*' and '*Minhaj*'. Whatever difference there exists between one religion and another is a difference in '*Shar'a*' and '*Minhaj*' and not a difference in '*Din*'. Thus, what matters is devotion to God and righteous living and the *Quran*, therefore, lays great emphasis upon tolerance.

Again through an interpretation of the *Quran*, Maulana Azad raises the question of group formations or groupism which had divided men into races, classes and nations, which had created differences between rich and poor, strong and weak, high and low, and so on. In the '*Surat-al-Fatiha*', it is stated that the urge for group formation was so strong that each group carved out for itself, separate places for worship. For example, Jews drew a circle around them and called it Judaism. Christians drew around themselves a circle and called it Christianity and any person outside this circle would not attain salvation. Maulana Azad says that the primary aim of every religion including the *Quran*, was the unity of man. But the followers of each religion discarded this message and every race raised groupism to the position of religion. Maulana Azad cites an example of how 'Baptism', which was merely a Jewish ceremonial, was converted by the Christian Church into an instrument of salvation. To this groupism and sectarianism, the *Quran*'s answer was that religion lies in strictly following the moral law prescribed by God and not in creating separate and conflicting groups. The word for goodness in the *Quran* is '*ma'aruf*', and for evil, '*munkar*'. The basis for all religions was one and the same — certain things are universally good and certain things universally bad. Maulana Azad's tolerance towards other religions was well reflected in his personality. The '*Din*' was not meant to divide man from man but to instill in them the feeling of fellowship. It was stressed in the *Quran* that if every group abides by this basic teaching of each religion, i.e. '*Din*', the disputes could be sorted out.

The *Quran* calls this Straight Path, the Path or '*Din*' of God as '*Sirat-al-Mustaqim*' which aims to bring together humanity and restore unity. The true follower of the *Quran* is one who treads this Straight Path. This beauty and mercy of God and the universal humanity reflected in the '*Surat-al-Fatiha*' finds itself well-embedded in the personality of Maulana Azad and he remains a symbol of the Muslim will to coexist peacefully in a religiously diverse country like India.

REFERENCES

1. Maulana Abul Kalam Azad, *The Tarjuman al-Quran*, (in Urdu), Volume One, *Surat-ul-Fatiha* (ed.), and rendered into English by Syed Abdul Latif, 1st Edition, 1962, 2nd Edition, 1965, 3rd Edition, 1981.
2. *The Quran*, translated by Abdullah Yusuf Ali, Goodword Books, 2010, Introduction, pp. vi-xiv.
3. Maulana Abul Kalam Azad, *Communal Harmony and Nationalism*, Presidential Address, Special Congress Session, Delhi, September 1923.

INDEX

Ahimsa, 63–64
Ajad ki Kahani Khud Azad, 28
Al-Balagh, 12–13, 22, 28–29, 32, 34, 37
Al-Hilal, 3, 9, 12–13, 22, 28–29, 31–38, 42–43, 48, 62–63
Aligarh Muslim University, 7, 10
Aligarh University, 36
Allah's Divine Justice, 69
Allied forces, 48–49
Al-Nadwa, 35
Anjuman-e-Islamia, 23
Anti-British movement, 21
Aristocratic leadership, 22
Assassination of Mahatma Gandhi, 10
Azad Ki Kahani Azad Ki Zubani, 43

Basic education, 59
Bengal Presidency, 4
Bengali Bhadralok, 4
Bengali intelligentsia, 8
Brahmanic religion, 70
British imperialism, 12, 17, 22, 31, 33

Caliphate, 49–50
Cambridge University, 42
Central Khilafat Committee, 50
Central Ministry of Education, 59
Christian Faith, 7
Christianity, 70, 72
Civil Disobedience Movement, 24, 51
Colonial government, 6, 8, 21
Colonialism, 28
Communal
 harmony, 12, 25, 28
 riots, 15–16, 18
Comparative religion, 1
Conservative leaders, 31
Co-religionists, 36, 65
Corpus funds, 8
Cultural development, 56
Curriculum, 9, 23, 59–60

Dar-ul-Irshad, 48
Dar-ul-Islam, 43
Defence of India Act, 22
Democracy, 31, 57–58, 64
Democratization of education, 57
Discontentment, 64
Divine Providence, 67–68
Domination structure, 57

East Bengal, 47
Eastern India, 4
Education
 adult, 57–58
 character building, 57
 collective, 33
 content of, 55, 57
 elementary, 55, 57
 fundamental, 55
 health, 55
 indigenous, 5
 literary, 55, 58
 madrasa, 9
 political, 37

primary, 57
religious, 34
social, 55, 58
Educational arrangement, 55
Educational development, 61
Eminent educationist, 25, 61
English newspapers, 33, 47

First World War, 3, 8, 12, 42, 48
Foreign domination, 20, 42
Forgiveness, 69–70
Freedom-fighter, 12, 25
Freedom struggle, 24, 31–32, 50, 63, 66
Fundamental Right, 57

Global citizenship, 59
Government of India Act, 50
Groupism, 72

Hindu
Bengalis, 8
communalists, 14
community, 65
ideology, 70
-militia-Rama Sena, 18
-Muslim partnership, 45
-Muslim riots, 15
-Muslim unity, 2–3, 15–16, 18, 21–24, 36, 49–51, 62, 65
Hindu Mahasabha, 16, 18
Hindu Raj, 18
Hindu Sangathan, 15
Hinduism, 17, 44
Holy Quran, 71
Home Rule Movement, 30

India Council for Technical Education, 25, 59
India Nationalist Party, 17
Indian Council for Cultural Relations, 59
Indian Council for Social Sciences Research, 59
Indian Freedom Movement, 21
Indian freedom struggle, 48–50, 52, 63
Indian Institute of Science, 25, 59
Indian National Commission for Cooperation, 59
Indian National Congress, 3–4, 7, 9, 15, 21
Indian National Movement, 49, 67
Indian National Union, 17
Indian struggle for Independence, 44, 62–63
Intellectual crisis, 1–3
Interim government, 18, 24
Internationalism and Global Citizenship, 59
Iranian revolutionaries, 22, 30
Iraqi revolutionaries, 48
Islam, 2, 15, 17, 28, 31, 35, 37, 42–45, 48, 50, 64, 71
Islamic
learning, 54
modernism, 22
philosophy, 55
rhetoric, 41
theology, 1, 7, 9, 41

Jallianwala Bagh masscare, 13
Jamiat-i-Hizb-Allah, 43
Jihad, 43, 49, 71
Jinnah, Muhammad Ali, 14, 16, 18, 24, 36, 44, 51–52, 65, 68, 70–71
Journalism, 27-30, 32–33, 35, 37-38

aggressive, 32
modern, 29
Journalistic
endeavour, 34
ethics, 37
professionalism, 28
pursuits, 32
Judaic concept, 70

Kher Committee for Elementary Education, 55
Khilafat Movement, 2, 13, 27, 30, 33, 44, 49

League leaders, 17
League's Resolution, 12
Liberalism, 68, 71
Lifelong collaboration, 63
Linguistic contribution, 33

Madarsa, 23
Mahatma Gandhi, 3, 10, 42, 44–45, 62–63
Mass movement, 63
Ministry of Education, 58–59
Mohamaden Educational Conference (MEC), 9
Movement of independence, 45
Muslim
aristocracy, 5
elite, 4, 22
high cast, 23
innocent, 19
middle class, 21
of Bengal, 51
of Ranchi, 23
orthodoxy, 41
political inertia, 36
politics, 27–29, 31, 34
population, 29
profession, 5
protagonist, 45
reformer, 70
representation, 16
resentment, 22
theology, 1
Muslim League, 4, 10, 12, 18–19, 22, 24, 30, 37, 51–52, 65
Muslim Sangathan, 15

National Education Day, 25, 61
National Institute of Basic Education, 59
National Integration, 58
National Movement, 1, 12, 49
National policies, 51, 60–61
Nationalism, 3, 21–22, 28, 31, 34, 41–42, 44–45, 49, 58
advocacy of, 34
composite, 44–45
federative character of, 44
idea of, 44
narrow, 59
territorial, 42
Nationalist
approach, 35
historiography, 7
leaders, 49
politics, 34
Nazism, 18
Nehru, Jawaharlal, 3, 14, 16
Nehru, Motilal, 15
Non-Cooperation Movement, 13–14, 24, 49, 63–64
Non-violence, 18

Obscurantism, 33–34

Paigam, 32
Pakistan Resolution, 16, 36

Pan-Islam, 2, 41–43, 45
Partition of Bengal, 8, 12, 21, 34, 47, 49
Physical education, 60
Political
- activism, 42
- beliefs, 33
- career, 32
- concept, 44
- domination, 64
- duties, 64
- freedom, 64
- ideologies, 3
- leaders, 62
- leadership, 4, 10, 30, 34
- life, 30
- movements, 36, 64
- organizations, 4
- philosophy, 63
- reactionaries, 16
- theory, 64
- unconsciousness, 37

Politics
- communal, 19, 28, 65
- revolutionary, 62
- separate, 31, 34
- separatist, 63, 66
- *ulema*, 41

Post-partition communal violence, 55
Premier leadership, 19
Presidential address, 18
Press Act, 32
Prophet Muhammad, 42

Quit India resolution, 24
Quran, 1, 32, 35, 41–43, 47–48, 51, 67–73

Racial discrimination, 13, 62
Rai, Lajpat, 14
Ramgarh Session, 17, 24
Rationalism, 31, 35, 56
Red Fort, 19
Religion-cultural habits, 41
Religious
- beliefs, 49
- bigotry, 31
- colour, 7
- enthusiasm, 42
- faith, 17, 42
- inactivity, 37
- institutions, 6
- leaders, 47, 49–50
- life, 33
- sanctity, 7
- separatism, 24
- symbolism, 32, 37

Revolutionary
- group, 43
- movements, 63

Rububiyat, 67–68

Salvation, 56, 72
Satyagraha Movement, 13
Secondary Education Commissions, 25, 55, 59
Separatist leadership, 36
Social history, 2
Surat-ul-Fatiha, 67, 69
Swadeshi Movement, 12, 30

Tabig and Tanzim movements, 15
Tarjuman-ul-Quran, 1, 23, 67, 72
Traditional beliefs, 41
Two Nation Theory, 19, 24, 65

UNESCO, 59–60
University Education Commission, 55

Urdu
  journalism, 27, 31–33, 37
  literature, 48
  newspaper, 42
  poetry, 47

Voice of Truth, 29

Wahabi Movement, 34
War policies, 48
Whadat-e-Adyan, 42

Zikr-e-Azad, 43